FLIGHT OF

FLIGHT OF FAITH

MY MIRACLE ON THE HUDSON

FREDERICK BERRETTA

Typeset and published in 2009 by Saint Benedict Press, LLC.
Typography is the property of Saint Benedict Press, LLC, and may not be
reproduced in whole or in part without written permission from the publisher.

ISBN: 978-1-935302-308

Cover design by Tony Pro.
Cover image © Associated Press, Photo/Steven Day

Printed and bound in the United States of America.

SAINT
BENEDICT
PRESS

Saint Benedict Press, LLC
Charlotte, North Carolina
2009

TABLE OF CONTENTS

I dedicate this book to the mercy of God, to the flight crew of U.S. Airways Flight 1549, to all who participated in the rescue of the passengers, and to the aeronautical engineers of the Airbus A-320.

And to my mother, who asked me to write this.

PREFACE

Shortly after takeoff from New York on January 15, 2009, a U.S. Airways Airbus A-320 crash-landed in the Hudson River. All 155 passengers and crew survived the crash and were rescued from the freezing waters within minutes. It was a unique event in the modern commercial jet era, and one that inspired hope and awe in millions who followed the news on television and radio.

Within an hour after the passengers and crew of Flight 1549 had safely debarked rescue boats, the governor of New York proclaimed, "We've had a Miracle on Thirty-fourth Street, and now I believe we've had a Miracle on the Hudson."

For the majority of the passengers, no such proclamation was needed. As a passenger on the flight (and as a private pilot) I had a profound appreciation for the feat that had been accomplished. Captain Chesley Sullenberger coolly and decisively set the plane down in a busy waterway, skillfully avoiding watercraft of various kinds. The airframe stayed intact after impact and floated long enough for ferryboats to arrive to pluck passengers from the wings and rafts, saving us from certain hypothermia and potential death. And the list goes on.

When I climbed up the ladder of the ferryboat *Thomas Jef-ferson*, two men waited at the top like sentinels of mercy, and helped me onto the deck. They patted each one of us on the back and told us we had made it and were okay. It was then that an overwhelming and indescribable sense of gratitude came over my being – a sense of gratitude to God and to all those who had saved my life and the lives of everyone on board the plane.

Shortly after the crash, I found myself being interviewed on CNN, Fox News, NPR, and several radio programs. And once I returned home, the questions kept coming: "How has this event affected you?" "Has your life changed?" "Did you pray on the flight?" "Do you believe it was a miracle?" In this account, I will try to answer those questions as thoughtfully as I can.

In myriad ways, Flight 1549 profoundly impacted my life perspective and my own faith journey. Though I find it diffi-cult to discuss my experiences so openly, I feel almost obligated to do so, driven by a profound gratitude. My faith helped me in critical moments during Flight 1549, and Flight 1549 for-ever transformed my faith. In a way, they are now inextricably linked together. The value of this story has little to do with me, but if, in the sharing of it, a single individual soul is inspired to deepen his trust in God, it will have been worth the effort.

Frederick Berretta

ACKNOWLEDGMENTS

I want to thank my relatives, friends, and colleagues who reached out to me following the crash landing of Flight 1549. Your thoughtful remarks will always be remembered and I am forever grateful.

To Adam Reiss and those whom I met at CNN and Fox News studios: thank you for your warm welcome after the crash.

To Bob Diforio: thank you for your encouragement, diligence, and belief in my ability to write my story. To Jamie Saloff, thank you for your direction. And to Todd Aglialoro for your patient guidance.

To Robert Allard, Dr. Art Bolz, Felix Carroll, Patrick Coffin, Rico De Silva, Father Anthony Gramlich, Deacon Brian Miller, Bhavit Patel, Gary Towery, Michele Wells, Christine Valentine-Oswik, James Hetzel, and all those whom I met who encouraged me to tell my story.

A special note of thanks to Vinny Flynn: I am glad I bought your book and very grateful for your inspiring help.

To my sisters, Michele and Tina: thank you for all of your

support. And to Bishop George Thomas: thank you for your prayers and counsel.

To my wife, Liz, and the four stars of our lives: Jonathan, Evan, Lauren, and Benjamin. It is for you that I have traveled to the corners of the world, and it is for you that I live my life. I am grateful to God that I have more time to be with you.

Finally, to Our Lady of the Bright Hill, the Star of the Sea, the humble Mother of God. You are the resplendent Queen of many titles, and you were with us over the waters of the Hudson that day. I hope to spend an eternity singing your praises for leading me to your Son, and for all you have done for me throughout my life.

CHAPTER 1

DECISION

Deep calls to deep in the roar of thy torrents. All thy
waves and breakers sweep over me.

Psalm 42: 8.

The morning of January 14, 2009, began like any other, as I made my way to work in morning traffic, although the bright clearness of the early sky contrasted with the melancholy of the state of the world. The news on the radio told of the uncertainty of war, of spiraling economic indicators and a deepening recession, and it pushed my mind to a place where I did not want to go. I grew tired of the back-and-forth bickering of journalists debating whether we were headed for another Great Depression, so I tuned out the chatter and thought about what I needed to get done in the day ahead.

As I tried to keep my patience in the midst of the painstaking creep that is the morning commute to uptown Charlotte, I had no idea that in a just few short hours I would be rushing to catch a flight to New York for a last-minute meeting. On practically a weekly basis I had been traveling to New York finishing up a series of projects, but I was not scheduled to go that week, and I was pleased to have a somewhat normal routine at home. My only regret that morning was that I had skipped my early morning prayer and meditation. I resolved to make up for it later on, recalling my New Year's resolution to commit more fully to my spiritual life and my relationship with God.

After making a few calls and arranging for an afternoon meeting with colleagues in New York, I decided that it would be important for me to attend in person. Critical decisions were being made regarding fellow associates' jobs, and I knew the discussions would be better face-to-face. I asked my assistant to quickly check flights as I multitasked, replying to emails and gathering materials for the trip. On most trips to New York, I'd usually returned on an evening flight. But when my assistant walked into my office and asked my preference, as all flights had open seats, I asked her to book the 2:45 p.m. return. I wanted to get home in time to see my kids before bed, at least this one week.

I hurried home to pack for the quick overnight trip. Over the years, I had traveled so much that I had grown to despise carrying an extra piece of luggage; I simply used my briefcase as a suitcase for overnight trips. I rushed to fold an extra suit and change of clothes, and shot out the door. I gave my wife a kiss and a hug, and I recall the house being very peaceful and quiet, and wishing that I could just stay home and forget the whole thing. I had spent a great deal of my professional life flying around the United States and abroad, yet each time there was a mental hurdle to overcome when I made my way to the airport. This time I also had a strange, uneasy feeling about the trip – due to concern over the meetings, I told myself – but I shook off the anxiety and headed out.

* * *

The weather was clear but very cold when I landed in New York and made my way into Manhattan. I had about twenty minutes before my first meeting, and I recalled my resolution to make up for my missed morning prayers. I knew that somewhere in my briefcase I had a small prayer book, and I decided to organize the inner pocket, which was full of personal items and papers, as I looked for it.

When I removed paperwork and emptied the contents of my briefcase, I found two old prayer booklets in a side pocket. I glanced over each. One, a little booklet called the *Pietà*, after the famous Michelangelo sculpture; contained a variety of devotional prayers, some of them many centuries old. Its cover was long missing and its pages worn thin. The other was a small volume on the Divine Mercy Chaplet. On the cover was an image of Christ with two rays of light shining out from his chest, one red and the other white. The booklet contained excerpts from a diary kept by a Polish nun in the 1930s, Saint Maria Faustina Kowalska, who claimed to have had visions of Christ and even dialogue with Him. Over the years I had prayed this simple chaplet off and on, but it had been many months since I had last prayed it. So I opened it up.

The book contains many passages from Saint Faustina's diary, but that day one in particular captivated me. At the three o'clock hour, she records Christ telling her, "I will refuse nothing to the soul that makes a request of Me in virtue of My Passion." As it happened to be just after three o'clock, I reflected on that and began to pray the chaplet. I prayed slowly and with great intensity, in a way that was unusual for me.

For the sake of His sorrowful Passion
Have mercy on me, and on the whole world.

I proceeded through my meetings, which went well, and had dinner with a work colleague. The next morning, I headed back downtown to connect with other associates. It was very cold, and the sky was overcast, with a light snow falling. I wondered if my afternoon flight would be canceled or delayed, as I continued with more meetings.

Just before noon after an unsuccessful attempt to connect with an associate for lunch, I got into a cab and made my way to the airport. We passed near Saint Patrick's Cathedral, between Madison Avenue and Fifth, and I asked the cabdriver to drop me there. I entered the beautiful old neo-Gothic church right as midday Mass was starting. After receiving Communion I felt compelled to light a candle in one of the side chapels, and I said the Prayer of Saint Patrick standing below his crystal reliquary.

As I was exiting the cathedral, I saw a gift shop just across the side street. I had a little time before my next conference call, which I would take in the cab, so I went in and browsed around. It was a small shop, with statues and icons and other religious items. Toward the back was a hallway where there were a few rows of books for sale. I glanced over the books and one title caught my eye: *7 Secrets of the Eucharist*, by Vinny Flynn. It seemed to be a small book that I could read in one sitting – perfect for the two-hour flight home, I thought.

I left the shop, headed to the corner of Fifth Avenue, and hailed a cab. By the time I finished my call I had arrived at LaGuardia Airport. I printed my boarding pass – I was reserved in seat 16A, a window seat on the left side of the plane, just behind the wing – and proceeded through security. I had time for a quick lunch, and as I sat waiting for my food I looked out the window and was relieved to see that the weather had cleared up completely. Inevitably, it seemed, flights from LaGuardia were delayed for one reason or another, but the lack of cloud cover would give us a better chance of departing on schedule. I finished eating and headed over to the gate, where, sure enough, boarding was about to begin more or less on time. I spent a few minutes in the pages of the book I'd purchased, and then it was my turn to board.

* * *

I found my row and placed my suit jacket and topcoat in the upper bin. Settling in my window seat, I checked a few more emails, replied to some, and then shut off my BlackBerry. Normally, I put my BlackBerry in my briefcase while flying, but this time I just slid it into my left pocket. From my briefcase I removed a work file, which I slid into the magazine pouch, and *7 Secrets,* which I picked up and began reading where I had left off.

As I read I became engrossed in the book, and was thinking about how meager my spiritual life had become over the past few years when I heard a voice from the distant past call to me aloud: "Fred Berretta, not riding front of the bus anymore?" I looked up and saw a stout man named Jim whom I had worked with years before. His familiar, slightly raspy voice took me back several years and I said, "I don't travel quite as much as I used to, so I lost my Chairman Preferred status, but it's fine with me." We both laughed and nodded, and as he made his way to the back of the plane, we agreed to catch up sometime in Charlotte.

The normal routine of aircraft boarding continued. Passengers found their seats, placed their belongings here and there, and the flight attendants made their rounds. Announcements were made, and the ritual I had seen and heard so many times before faded away as I focused my mind back on my book.

The doors were finally closed, we began to move back from the Jetway, and I looked out the window to see if I could gauge how many aircraft were approaching the runway, hoping we wouldn't have too long a wait. I continued reading. The taxi seemed to take about twenty minutes or so, and at that point I had read through over half the book. Deciding that I should take a break and reflect on what I had just read, as it seemed rather profound to me, I put the book away and closed my eyes.

The pilot came over the speaker and told us we were next in line for takeoff. The usual sound of the engines spooling filled the plane, I felt the welcoming force of the seat thrusting me forward, and we began our roll. The part of any flight I always enjoyed the most was takeoff, even though as a pilot I knew it was the most dangerous part. It was always the most exciting part of the ride, watching the world below dwindle to minia-ture as we lifted into the skies.

The wheels lifted off Runway 4 and we climbed in a north-easterly vector, and I heard the familiar sound of the landing gear retracting, followed by the *clunk* of the gear tucking itself into the wings. The takeoff felt smooth and perfectly normal, and I reclined slightly to make a little more room to adjust to the confinement of a coach window seat.

I meditated on the insights from my new book, and felt more and more relaxed. I had never been able to sleep on planes, but I could manage to get into a calm state that was about halfway to unconsciousness. I liked that feeling, as it allowed for the kind of reflection that was difficult during the course of a nor-mal busy day.

3:24:58 LaGuardia Tower: "Cactus fifteen forty-nine."

3:25:51 Captain Sullenberger: "Cactus fifteen forty-nine, seven hundred climbing five thousand."

3:26:00 Air Traffic Control: "Cactus fifteen forty-nine New York departure, radar contact, climb and maintain one five thou-sand."

3:26:04 Captain Sullenberger: "Maintain one five thousand, Cactus fifteen forty-nine."

I went deeper and deeper into my relaxing sojourn, thinking about points the author had touched on regarding the Eucharist, and how mysterious they were. The hum of aircraft sounds nudged me to close my eyes. My mind moved back and forth between work, my family, the noon Mass at Saint Patrick's, the book I had been reading, and I drifted into a tranquil, almost dreamlike state.

Then I was jolted violently from my restfulness by a noise I had never heard before on a plane.

It was a kind of thud, as if something had impacted the fuselage somewhere, but exactly what it was or where it hit, I couldn't tell. I thought I heard it come from the left, but it also seemed to be everywhere at the same time. For a few instants the plane shook violently from side to side, and then it settled. My eyes snapped open and my mind instantly tried to process what had just happened.

Fear tried to penetrate my emotions, but I fought it back. I turned my head to look out the window, hoping that the engine was still there: for the only thing I could guess was that somehow, as unlikely as it might be, it had sheared by itself and fallen off the wing. But through the window there was the wing, intact, and the engine – in flames. My mind frantically searched for answers in my aviation knowledge; my faith was shrouded in a fog of dread that had begun to encompass my whole being.

In the next few moments I would begin the longest, shortest journey of my life. The moments would stretch out like a dream, and I would recall the distant years, the entirety of my existence, and I would have to reconcile myself to them – and to God. The moments I thought would be the last of my life.

CHAPTER 2

SEARCH

"We can lift ourselves out of ignorance, we can find ourselves as creatures of excellence and intelligence and skill. We can be free! We can learn to fly!"

From *Jonathan Livingston Seagull*, by Richard Bach

From my earliest memories as a child, I loved aircraft and anything to do with flying. I remember vividly my first flight on a Delta Airlines DC-8. My father showed me the wings and engines, and the pilots invited me up to the cockpit after takeoff. This love affair continued into space as well, and I remember watching various Apollo missions on television and wondering what it would be like to fly to the moon.

My family moved to southeast Florida in 1969, and as the youngest of three siblings and the only boy, I received a lot of attention from my parents. If you asked either of my older sisters, they of course would claim I was spoiled. Indeed, even though I have debated this subject with them on many occasions, I yield to their assertion that I enjoyed a special popularity; but it would be short-lived.

By the early seventies, the era of martini lunches was in full swing. I of course was not enjoying martinis myself, but it seemed my parents were always occupied with a cocktail party or social event of some kind. Yet it was still a time when children could ride their bikes all day in the neighborhood and parents did not have to worry about their safety. The few channels on television were not the epicenter of activity. Yes, I can look back and say that for a short while I lived a picturesque American family life – but it was not to last. There were moments of laughter, fun, and even joy in our household, but my sisters and I sensed there was something dreadfully wrong. My parents' relationship had been strained for several years, and recently they had been fighting more frequently and intensely, filling our home with an atmosphere of deep anxiety. My sisters and I never knew when the next verbal battle would take place, and we felt helpless to do anything about it. Right around my eighth birthday, it was all over.

When the day finally came, I remember my parents gathering me and my sisters in the living room of our home by the waterway, with its red velvet carpet, white chairs, black sofa, enigmatic paintings, all in the shadow of a baby grand piano. (Yes, this was the seventies – the decade when interior designers must have been launched into space with the Apollo astronauts.) It was highly unusual for them to arrange a family discussion in such a formal manner. With the instincts of a young child I somehow knew when we sat down that the conversation would forever change my life. My parents looked at each other and then at us, and then my mother explained that she and my father were getting divorced. I remember thinking that it had something to do with me, that somehow it was my fault. They assured me it was not, but that didn't make it any easier.

* * *

My sisters ultimately went on to live with my father and I stayed with my mother. We existed in a state of uncertainty and financial instability much of the time, and I had to change schools frequently. I would visit my father on weekends and during the summers, and with few friends, I had to lean on my imagination to fill the void that had come into my impressionable life.

My family was nominally Catholic: we had attended Mass on Sundays, or at least most Sundays. My father was raised Catholic and my mother Methodist, but she had practiced Catholicism for a short while prior to the divorce. On occasion we said a blessing before dinner, but we never prayed consistently as a family, and during the months that led up to my parents' separation, all forms of devotional activity completely ceased. Through it all, though, I always held onto a belief in God, however simple. I had an awareness of good and evil in the world that was beyond the human person, and I saw the two forces play out in the breakup of my family life. In the aftermath my mind and heart began the search for a greater reality, something permanent and reliable that I could cling to for hope, that would restore what I had lost. I blamed the presence of evil for the destruction of my family security, and in my childlike manner I vowed I would do all I could to fight that very evil.

Ironically, when as a young child my family was still together and going to Mass, I attended various Protestant denominational schools, but after the divorce, when neither of my parents practiced the Faith, I attended Catholic schools and received the sacraments. And as I grew into adolescence, I began to form my own devotional approach to God. I recall at night making the sign of the cross and saying informal prayers to God for protection. On Sundays I rode my bike to a local Catholic church and for a short while participated as an altar server.

In my efforts to free my mind from the lack of stability of my life, I continued to develop my love of flight, and took an interest in science fiction, and these two things became my outlet in my search for inner freedom. One of the places we lived happened to be in the flight path of Ft. Lauderdale-Hollywood International Airport. As the commercial jets approached for landing, they passed just a few thousand feet above. I used to sit outside and watch them for hours, one after the other, with their whining turbines as they made descent.

I began reading all I could on aircraft and flying, and soon I knew every make of airliner by type. When we moved to Palm Beach a couple of years later, once again we lived directly under an airport flight path, and I could watch the jets on their takeoff ascent just as they headed out over the Atlantic. I often stood on a deserted beach and looked up at them and dreamed of being a pilot. To me at that time, there was no occupation in the world more noble or exciting.

* * *

Like many children who grow up without stability in school and the home, I was a shy boy. I spent a lot of time alone, and had to rely on my creativity for entertainment. Television in the days before cable offered few options, video games had not been developed yet, and there were few convenient sports opportunities for me. So I read books, any books I could find.

One day I recall coming home and telling my mom I had to write a report on a book I had not yet read. She was too tired to take me to the library, where I wanted to check out a book on space travel. I was reluctant therefore when she came into my room and handed me a slim paperback with a haunting image of a white gull on its dark blue cover: *Jonathan Livingston Seagull,* by Richard Bach. It was a far cry from space travel, but as I had no choice and the book report was due soon, I began reading. In many respects, it was a fateful gift that sparked my quest for a greater meaning to life.

The story was a simple one: a seagull named Jonathan Livingston becomes an outcast because he loves to fly; whereas all good and obedient seagulls in the flock were supposed to fly in order only to eat and survive. Any aspiration to a higher form of flying was forbidden. Once I started reading the book, I couldn't put it down. When I finished it, I read it again until I fell asleep on the floor in my room. I could identify with Jonathan: I was an outcast too, in a broken family, with few friends to play with. I also loved flight, and I could almost feel what it was like to fly as I read those pages over and over and gazed at the black-and-white pictures of seagulls inside. Not only did the book feed my passion for flight, but it also awakened in me a deeper view of life. Jonathan's progression as a flier is mirrored by personal growth, and as he becomes a teacher and leader of other gulls, he comes to learn that the only thing more important than flying is love.

* * *

By the time I was a teenager, I had moved in with my father. My sisters were both married and had long left home. My passion for flight and science fiction were now being supplemented with typical teenage activities: school, sports, music, and sharing my newly acquired wisdom with my father. During this time I also left behind my childhood views of God, though I never gave up on my beliefs entirely, even though I no longer attended Mass or practiced any regular forms of devotion.

When I was sixteen, one day after playing several tennis matches back to back, I was walking back home and felt a tremendous pain in my side. I thought it might be dehydration or perhaps a strained muscle. It grew worse and then subsided, but I became extremely ill with flu-like symptoms of high fever, nausea, and fatigue. By the third day of this ordeal I wasn't any better, so my Dad took me to the doctor. After checking me over for about ten minutes, the doctor said I most likely had a ruptured appendix, and rushed me to the hospital. I found myself on a metal gurney and felt the prick of a needle and then was asked to count backward from ten seconds down. I made it to about five seconds and was out.

When I awoke many hours later, I saw a nun standing next to me with a Rosary in her hand. She was smiling and told me I was a fortunate boy. She did not say much, but just handed me a cup of water. After a few more minutes of silent prayer, she left the room. Shortly afterward, my parents came in and my mother indicated that she had prayed for me on her way to the hospital. This was surprising to me, and I knew my situation must have been very serious.

Indeed, the doctor had told my parents I was very lucky. Severe peritonitis, an infection of the abdominal cavity, had localized from my ruptured appendix, and he said I was within a few hours of certain death. He told me he was amazed I had gone three days in this state and lived.

I didn't know whether it was by prayer, God's grace, or good fortune, but I had narrowly escaped death. Not for the last time.

* * *

I graduated with honors from a respected private secular high school, and for a brief period I considered enlisting in the Air Force and becoming a fighter pilot. But for reasons I do not wholly recollect, I felt at the time that a military career was not for me. Instead I chose business. It was the eighties, the era of investment banking, Wall Street stardom, and alternative music, and I gave my devotion to these ends.

I can see now that in my youth God had never stopped calling to me, even in the midst of family tumult. He called to me as a child at night, when I felt the inclination to make the sign of the cross and ask for protection. He called to me as a boy when I participated in Mass, and while I gazed at the sea as I made my way back home from church. He called to me as a teenager when I lay within hours of death, and during the long, painful nights of recovery in a hospital bed. His voice had constantly pursued me in whispers through the stages of my young life. At times I had hearkened to his call; but now I stopped listening, and I chose to let the spirit of the world overtake me.

CHAPTER 3

SILENCE

The only other sound's the sweep
Of easy wind and downy flake.
The woods are lovely, dark and deep,
But I have promises to keep,
And miles to go before I sleep.

From "Stopping by Woods on a Snowy Evening",
by Robert Frost

C old silence penetrated the air as I stared hypnotized at the exhaust cone of the left engine. It was on fire, and emitting a dark, foul-looking trail of smoke. I thought at any second it would just explode, or cause the wing, full of highly flammable jet fuel, to ignite.

3:27:32 Air Traffic Control: "Cactus fifteen forty-nine turn left heading two seven zero."
3:27:36 Captain Sullenberger: "Ah, this is uh cactus fifteen thirty-nine [sic]. Hit birds. We lost thrust in both engines. We're turning back towards LaGuardia."

3:27:42 Air Traffic Control: "Okay yeah you need to return to LaGuardia. Turn left heading of, uh two two zero."

3:27:46 Captain Sullenberger: "Two two zero."

3:27:49 Air Traffic Control: "Tower, stop your departures we got an emergency returning . . ."

3:27:53 LaGuardia Tower: "Who is it?"

3:27:54 Air Traffic Control: "It's fifteen twenty-nine [sic]. He ah, bird strike he lost all engines. He lost the thrust in the engines he is returning immediately."

3:27:59 LaGuardia Tower: "Cactus fifteen twenty-nine [sic] . . . WHICH engines?"

3:28:01 Air Traffic Control: "He lost thrust in both engines he said."

3:28:03 LaGuardia Tower: "Got it."

I looked back and across the cabin. The other passengers were bewildered and tense, but patiently awaiting an update from the pilot. I could not imagine what had caused a catastrophic failure of the left engine, and I turned my eyes back to it through the window and just stared, completely dumbfounded. Then I became aware of the smell of smoke and fuel in the plane. Could there be an electrical fire in the cabin, too?

The plane started to level off and make a left turn, gradual at first, then more pronounced. I continued my fixation on the engine, as if staring at it could keep it from exploding. Passengers were asking each other what was going on, not frantically yet, but with rising intensity. I looked at the man to my right and indicated that we had lost the left engine, and he craned his neck to try and see it from his middle seat. I turned back and just kept staring at it, thinking that any second the captain would tell us what had happened, that we had lost an engine, and that we were making our way safely back to LaGuardia.

*3:28:05 Air Traffic Control: "Cactus fifteen twenty-nine [sic],
if we can get it to you do you want to try to land runway one three?"*
   *3:28:11 Captain Sullenberger: "We're unable. We may end up
in the Hudson."*

I was inwardly shaken, but made a conscious effort to remain
calm. I knew that all twin-engine commercial airliners, including the Airbus A-320, could fly on one engine. I kept telling
myself, *Okay, we've lost the left engine, and we're going to make
an emergency landing. We still have the right engine, and we'll be
fine.*

We continued to bank to the left, then leveled off, and then
I heard something else I had never heard on a plane before:

Silence.

There was no engine roar or vibration, just the faintest hint
of the wind passing by outside, and perhaps a very slight puff-
ing noise, ever so soft, coming from the left engine. I turned
my head toward the aisle and tried to get the attention of the
man in seat 16F, the window seat on the right side of the aircraft. I called out to him, "What's going on over there? Can
you see anything? Is the right engine making noise? Can you
hear anything? We've lost the left engine."

He looked out the window, looked back toward me, and
then looked out again. He shook his head, "I don't hear anything."

The plane was gradually descending, gliding through the
air in the strange, ubiquitous silence. It was stable, but going
down steadily, and I knew by our heading we were not pointed
toward any airport.

At that moment, I felt a surge of something in my blood,
perhaps adrenaline, perhaps fear, but nothing that made me
feel good. It was as if an unseen force were compressing me,
and pulling me down into my seat; a wave of dread that went

through me and also originated within me. It was oppressive and all-consuming, and I had to work to fight off the temptation of terror and panic as I looked out my window again and then at the men to my right. We were just stunned, sitting there in that eerily quiet atmosphere of doom.

3:28:31 Air Traffic Control: "*All right, Cactus fifteen forty-nine it's going to be left traffic three one.*"

3:28:34 Captain Sullenberger: "*Unable.*"

3:28:36 Air Traffic Control: "*Okay, what do you need to land?*"

3:28:46 Air Traffic Control: "*Cactus fifteen forty-nine runway four is available if you want to make left traffic to runway four.*"

3:28:50 Captain Sullenberger: "*I am not sure we can make any runway. Oh what's over to our right, anything in New Jersey, maybe Teterboro?*"

3:28:55 Air Traffic Control: "*Okay, yeah off to your right side is Teterboro Airport . . . Do you want to try and go to Teterboro?*"

3:29:03 Captain Sullenberger: "*Yes.*"

3:29:05 Air Traffic Control: "*Teterboro, uh empire actually LaGuardia departure got an emergency inbound.*"

3:29:10 Teterboro Tower: "*Okay, go ahead.*"

3:29:11 Air Traffic Control: "*Cactus fifteen twenty-nine [sic] over the George Washington Bridge wants to go to the airport right now.*"

3:29:14 Teterboro Tower: "*He wants to go to our airport, check. Does he need any assistance?*"

3:29:17 Air Traffic Control: "*Ah yes, he ah, he was a bird strike can I get him in for runway one?*"

3:29:19 Teterboro Tower: "*Runway one, that's good.*"

3:29:21 Air Traffic Control: "*Cactus fifteen twenty-nine [sic] turn right two eight zero. You can land runway one at Teterboro.*"

3:29:25 Captain Sullenberger: "*We can't do it.*"

3:29:26 Air Traffic Control: "*Okay, which runway would you like at Teterboro?*"

3:29:28 Captain Sullenberger: "We're gonna be in the Hudson."

3:29:33 Air Traffic Control: "I'm sorry, say again Cactus."

I tried to make out LaGuardia Airport, which I knew had to be somewhere to the left and approaching. The city below us was getting larger; it seemed we were right on top of the roofs of buildings. I felt incredulous at it all, stupefied, almost in denial. I could not imagine what had knocked out both engines.

I knew we couldn't be far from the airport, but we kept descending inexorably toward the city skyline, and I still could not make out anything that resembled a runway. Just then the plane made what I recall to be a descending right turn, and we were squarely over the Hudson River. I heard the distinctive sound of the flaps extending a notch. The captain had still not said anything to us yet, and it seemed as though an eternity had passed, even though it probably had been only a few minutes, perhaps no more than three.

3:29:51 Air Traffic Control: "Cactus, ah Cactus fifteen forty-nine radar contact is lost. You also got Newark Airport off your two o'clock and about seven miles."

3:30:06 Air Traffic Control: "Eagle flight forty-seven eighteen, turn left heading two one zero."

3:30:09 Eagle Flight 4718: "Two one zero, uh forty-seven eighteen. I don't know. I think he said he was going in the Hudson."

3:30:14 Air Traffic Control: "Cactus fifteen twenty-nine [sic], uh you still on?

As the river approached, the voice we anticipated with every fiber of our beings – the one we would cling to for every answer to the questions in our frantic minds – finally came over the intercom. I still expected to hear some description of the engine failure, and that we would be making an emergency landing back at LaGuardia. I imagine most passengers expected a similar announcement.

The voice came, commanding but calm, intense but in control, and it uttered seven words:

"This is the captain, brace for impact."

We were not headed for any airport. I could see the water approaching, and the captain had said "impact," not "landing." I heard the faint cry of a female voice a few rows ahead of me, then another, and I heard a passenger in the row behind me ask, "Where are we landing? What's going on?"

I knew where we were going. I looked at the man to my right, and shook my head.

"We're going in the water."

He glanced out the window and then stared straight ahead. I saw the same look in his eyes that I knew was in mine: the full range of emotions captured in an instant, a window into the soul of a man facing his death.

* * *

I looked out at the city skyline and then at the wing. The water was closing in. I squinted to try to estimate our altitude, and wondered what a river ditching would feel like. Into my mind flashed images of the crash of an Ethiopian Airlines 767 off the coast of the Comoros Islands. Not two months prior, I had seen a television documentary on aviation disasters, and I remembered how that plane had careened across the ocean and broken into several pieces, killing most of the passengers on board. A video camera, operated by a vacationing tourist on the shore, caught the crash in the last few seconds. It had been horrifying to watch, and now the scene played over and over in my mind's eye.

I looked at the wing to see how steady it was, hoping we could at least enter the water at a level attitude. *Maybe we would have a chance*, I thought. *Maybe some of us.* I gave my-self a very optimistic fifty-fifty chance of survival, much less if the plane broke up badly. The passengers in the first few rows would have the best chance, for the most probable outcome was the plane would break apart a few rows behind the cock-pit and also behind the wing at the weak areas of the fuselage, right where I was sitting. The rear part of the aircraft would hit the water first and take the full force of the crash impact. The result would be a catastrophic breakup of the airframe and most of the passengers would be killed instantly or drowned within seconds.

A sweat broke out across my face and body, and I could feel my heart rate escalating. I glanced again at the men in my row, made eye contact, and thought I should say something. But what? We just looked at each other, with shocked stares, and then went into our own worlds, for whatever time we had left.

During those moments, the atmosphere on board the plane, the serene view of Manhattan, and the deep blue of the clear sky made everything seem peaceful in a strange way. I thought about my whole family, about my wife and four children, and my eyes started to water. I thought about how hard it would be for them, and how much I would miss them, and I felt so sad about leaving them. I just shook my head and looked down at my seatbelt, then closed my eyes.

My aviation experience could help me no longer as I sat mo-tionless, fighting fear and the overwhelming dissolution of en-ergy from the invisible force of dread. *I must turn to God now,* I thought to myself. *I must turn to my faith, however strong or weak it may be. I know it will be tested, perhaps beyond my capac-ity to accept. It will be put in the crucible and I must go there with it, hand in hand, as it leads me through the door that waits in the fog of this impossible situation. And I must go as the man that I am now, sitting here on this airplane, and not the one I wish to be someday. And I must not be afraid to go.*

Although I cannot say I witnessed my life flashing before my eyes, I did experience some variation of that. I thought about my life holistically – as a boy, an adolescent, and a man. My mind assimilated a mini self-judgment and life review. I had made a genuine effort to do my best, and had made mistakes. I had tried to be charitable and generous with my success and I had tried diligently to live my Catholic faith to its fullest, but I knew I could have done better, much better. I assessed my relationship with God and found it wanting. Yet, I had received the Sacrament of Reconciliation the prior weekend, and, earlier that day, Communion at Saint Patrick's. I was about as prepared to meet God as I could, but I still desperately wanted more time.

I pondered for a few moments the journey of my faith – how long it had taken to finally acquire it – and how much I had struggled to live it well. I sensed impending judgment; I knew that I would be facing each of my life decisions as I emerged through death's door, and I wondered what I had amounted to in the eyes of God. So many times I had run away from Him and toward the distractions of the world. Now I could run no longer. In my mind everything was crashing down on me – the good and the bad I'd done, the joys and the hopes I'd had, the victories I'd won and the setbacks I'd suffered – as I sat there in the silent machine that in a moment would become my lifeboat or my coffin.

CHAPTER 4

METANOIA

I fled Him, down the nights and down the days,
I fled Him, down the arches of the years,
I fled Him, down the labyrinthine ways
Of my own mind; and in the mist of tears
I hid from Him.

From "The Hound of Heaven," by Francis Thompson

When I entered college, I abandoned religion. In fact, my movement away from the Church had begun during the last two years of high school, as I yielded to the secularized environment at home and at school. By the time I was a freshman in college, academic demands, fraternity life, weekend parties, and all the other temptations that came with living away from home all kept my mind far away from God and the Faith.

In addition to the casual, worldly circumstances of college life, it happened that each year some major event occurred that left me feeling anger toward God. In the first few weeks of my freshman year, a suitemate of mine was killed in a freak accident while playing touch football. He caught a pass and fell

while running, and the impact of hitting the ground with the
football pressed to his chest caused the separation of a critical
nerve to his heart. He stood up and then fell dead. I, along
with several other boys, gave him a eulogy in the chapel on
campus, and I remember distinctly in my heart blaming God
for the accident. He was the kindest and smartest soul in our
freshman suite of eight young men, and it was a sobering way
to begin my undergraduate years.

The next year, my mother's husband, to whom she'd been
married for twelve years, died suddenly of a heart attack, and
I worried whether she could make it without him. How could
God let that happen to my mother? In the middle of my ju-
nior year, my Dad's business failed and he could no longer pay
my college tuition, so I had to obtain student loans to get me
through. Finally, during senior year he had to leave our home
in southeast Florida, and it was as if the final chapter of my
youth had closed. All these events drove me to frustration toward God, and recalled again the old feeling that I couldn't
count on anything in my life to remain stable and secure.

For some reason, though, I always continued to believe in
God, however fragile or tenuous that belief was, for I reasoned
that the universe and its workings were far too complex to have
originated by pure chance. I suppose as well I held onto frag-
mented, romantic vestiges of my Catholic faith, in pieces and
vague memories that lingered in my mind. On very rare occasions, I can even say I prayed. But these moments were few and
indeed far between.

* * *

After graduating, I moved to Atlanta, and along with a college
friend I tried to start a software company. I worked three jobs
for almost a year before, exhausted and disillusioned, I gave
up on the business idea. Humbled, I settled for an entry-level
accounting position at a regional trust company. My life then

was probably typical of many recent college graduates: working during the week and partying on weekends. Tennis was a very popular sport in Atlanta, and as I had played in high school, it became a good outlet for exercise and socializing. After my college romance ended, I began casually dating and was set up on a few blind dates (all of which were utter failures!).

As seemingly pleasant as my life had become, I could feel something eating away at me, from deep inside: something I couldn't explain and didn't care to admit. It was a cynicism, an inner frustration and anxiety, fueled by a void of meaning in my life that at the time I didn't understand. I had also lost my interest in reading, as I grew increasingly unable to focus my attention on anything that required an investment of patience.

Then, one weekend afternoon, alone in my apartment, as I stared out the window at a line of trees behind a water reservoir, there came over me an urge to write. I thought of how lonely life could be, and how limited was the human soul's ability to help itself. The restlessness inside me just had to get out, so I took a pencil and a notebook and began to write. Over the next few weeks I sketched out a few poems, trying to put in words the strange torpor I felt inside. One in particular conveys my state of mind at the time, as I struggled to connect with every alienated soul in the world who may have felt the same longing I had:

A dreaded, deep and dreary sleep,
Befalls us slowly in its keep,
And in a hollow realm we weep –
And thus begins its way.
This in time becomes our course,
Nulled by existential force,
Encompassed in a shell remorse –
And hardens us each day.

Yet by our nature we should show
To those who might around us know,
Our wayward weakness, weary so –
To ask for help some way.
Still and silent we bide with fear,
From sharing what to us is dear,
To close the space between us near –
And far from those we stray.
Thus in the end we make our stress
A greater part of us than less,
We hold back what we should express –
And fall far, far away.

At this point you probably are considering consulting a team of psychiatrists to help lift your spirits. I completely understand. Pretty gloomy – and that's what I thought too, when I wrote them. Yet they somehow helped me come to terms with the mysterious sense of emptiness I felt, and for a while, writing made me feel better.

Over the next couple of years, I was able to move into another position with my company, but had to relocate to Charlotte. I had really started to enjoy my life in Atlanta, so moving was a difficult choice, but I felt it was the right career decision. And, I can see now, being away from my circle of friends and acclimating to a new job forced me to deal with my internal absence of peace and contentment.

Thinking exercise might be the answer, I began jogging around my neighborhood, even though I really did not care for running at all. I quickly worked up to about five miles a day. My weekends became solitary retreats; I might play an occasional tennis match, go for a run, and then sleep the rest of the weekend away.

* * *

One very hot afternoon, I returned to my apartment and sat down, discouraged as ever. My apartment was very quiet. For some reason – boredom, maybe, or the prompting of grace – I decided to look through a box in my closet that contained sentimental items from my childhood days. There I came across an old family bible. I scanned the pages and read a few lines here and there. It was a sad heirloom of lost days, and it reminded me of when my family was all together.

Then something came over me. I felt as though the door of my soul, long locked and held fast by my inner pride and cynicism, opened for just a moment. I put the bible down. I had been sitting on the floor next to my bed, and now I knelt there, folded my hands, and bowed my head. It was as if something inside my head was moving my limbs, directing me how to pray. I could not remember how long it had been since I had prayed like that – perhaps not since my very early childhood, perhaps never. I couldn't recall any prayer that I had learned in school, except the Lord's Prayer, and I struggled to remember all the words. I did not know how to pray or how to approach God personally. The only reference I had was gleaned from television evangelists, such as Billy Graham, who had taught the value of giving your life to Christ.

So I said the Lord's Prayer as best I could, and then I just began to speak honestly to God. I poured my heart and soul into that prayer, humbling myself, moving between asking God if He really existed to pleading for His help. Imperfect as my prayer and conversation with God were that day, it was all thoroughly contrite. I felt better afterward, though I did not know what to do next.

As the weeks progressed, I began spontaneously saying the Lord's Prayer in my head as I drove or ran. I even began reading from the Bible, and for brief moments I would tune in, captivated, to the Sunday evangelists on television. Around this same time I met my future wife, and we began dating. Life seemed to be heading on a better track. From time to time I would think about returning to Mass, but something held me back. I thought that I wasn't ready to be welcomed by God again. But in reality, though, it was only my pride and ego.

* * *

One weekend afternoon, I came across a television documentary about Fatima. The story centered on three young shepherd children, uneducated and poor, who lived in the hills of Portugal, near Lisbon. On May 13, 1917, they supposedly had seen the Mother of Jesus, who continued to appear to them on the same day of each month until October. The children initially were not believed and were even persecuted, but eventually some 70,000 people witnessed a supernatural phenomenon that would be called the "Miracle of the Sun." The children were also given a number of prophecies that would come to pass.

Although I had heard stories of apparitions of the Virgin Mary before, I'd tended to quickly dismiss them as delusions of overzealous piety. Yet this documentary made a deep impression on me. I felt drawn to the story of Fatima, and I read everything about it that I could find.

One day not long after, I was sitting in my office in a pensive mood. Lunchtime was approaching. Usually I ate at my desk and just worked through lunch; this day, however, I was moved to get up and find a Catholic church. It was an inner impulse that suddenly encompassed me, and it had a strange urgency to it, like a last-minute invitation to go on a faraway voyage that you have only a few moments to decide about.

I had not been in *any* church for years, but I immediately went to my car and began driving. I had recalled seeing a Catholic church somewhere near uptown Charlotte. After a short while I found Saint Patrick's, the cathedral church of Charlotte. I went into the church, which was empty and perfectly quiet. There were bright stained-glass windows depicting scenes from the gospel. I felt the peace of it envelop me, and I walked slowly to the altar, observing carefully each window as I passed by. I was taken by the myriad colors that came through the windows and shined down into the sanctuary.

I approached the tabernacle, where the Eucharist is reserved, stood before it for a moment, then knelt down. I thought about my life: my search for God, for some greater truth to guide my life by. I thought of how much time I had wasted, and how so many of my acts and attitudes must have offended God. I became aware of a deep clarity about my life, and a great sorrow for my past transgressions, and I began to weep silently. I could almost feel God's embrace, as I pondered the empty years. I knelt there for almost an hour, and when I left that church I knew I was somehow a changed man. A love for Christ and the Church and Christ had been infused – or rekindled – in my heart, and I wanted to learn as much as I could about my faith, and improve my life. I thought this experience might have been the answer to the prayer I had prayed months earlier, though I did not really understand what was happening to me.

I began reading books on theology, dozens of them. I read books on the saints and history of the Church. I also researched the origins of the Rosary, the ancient Christian devotion that I had first learned about through the Fatima documentary. Supposedly, there were fifteen promises made to those who prayed it with sincere devotion, and one in particular struck me: "Whoever shall recite the Rosary devoutly, applying himself to the consideration of its sacred mysteries, shall never be conquered by misfortune . . . nor perish by a bad death."

Although I was intrigued by this notion of promises, I admit that the whole idea of such an arrangement between God, through the Mother of Christ, and devout Christians seemed somewhat childish to me. But, I felt my experience was too profound to turn back and that I had to keep moving forward on faith alone, so I purchased a small booklet on the Rosary and I tried to pray. Around this time I also learned about the Chaplet of Divine Mercy, a devotional prayer with ordinary Rosary beads – which seemed very efficient to me. I made progress in my daily spiritual disciplines and found much clarity and consolation through them.

Liz and I married and I committed myself to doing all I could to live my faith well. I strove to accept and believe all that the Church taught. Those teachings I did not fully understand, I researched, questioned, and then reasoned through. They all made perfect sense to me, for I saw them as a mosaic, a deeply interlaid mix of critical and complimentary variation that could not be separated, because it was one thing. The beauty of it, I loved. The wisdom of it, I adored. At the depth of it, I marveled. I simply could not get enough of it. I was fortunate to have two honeymoons: one with my wife and one with the Catholic Church.

Liz and I had our first son in our first year of marriage, and our second son in our second year of marriage. Although overjoyed and grateful for our boys, we were both working, learning how to be married, and learning how to be parents in one crash course. We decided that although it would be financially challenging, it would be best for our sons if Liz stayed home and took care of them full time. The full weight of the financial burden was now on my shoulders, and although my zeal for my newfound faith gave me great strength and energy, the honeymoon phase for both my marriage and my conversion had ended. Our marriage no longer was focused on just us but on our boys, and work demanded ever more of my time and my energy.

* * *

The day I took my first business trip was a dim one. If at the time I'd had any notion of the extent of travel I would endure in the following years, I probably would have cried. With success in my job came more travel, and with travel came stress, and with more stress came a subtle, but palpable inner disillusionment. The situation was compounded by the fact that my wife did not share the same zeal for the Catholic faith as I did, and I couldn't understand why she had not had a similar conversion experience. I expected too much from her, and also was discouraged by my lack of ability to "talk her into" a more robust devotion which we could share together – that is, during those times when I was not traveling on business to the far corners of the world.

Liz was performing in a phenomenal manner as a wife and as a loving mother to our sons, and we were both learning about each other, and learning how to communicate effectively in the midst of the day-to-day struggles. It was naturally challenging for her to understand my zeal for the Catholic faith (as I did not fully grasp it either!) and it was understandably disappointing for me not to be on the same spiritual page as my wife.

With the compounding effect of increased workload, travel, and various stages of parenting, I began struggling to maintain the vibrancy of faith that had carried me through my conversion experience and early years of marriage. Somehow I had assumed that the feelings of contentment and fulfillment I had known in the early stages of my conversion would always be there, regardless of my situation or attitude. But although I made good progress and learned much about my faith, over time fatigue and stress began to dampen my zeal. Praying the Rosary had become a mere exercise and then a burden, a daily task that I began to dread more than enjoy. I was allowing the thorns of life to choke out my spirituality, and my mind was too much in the events of the world and on my work. My ego was being broken down and I was resisting the process, and in that resistance was my error.

I had asked and I had received. I had sought and I had

found. I had knocked and the door had been opened for me. I walked through the door and was mesmerized by what I saw. The Mother of God held my hand and led me to her Son and His teachings. My spirit had basked in the pure light of the realm of truth, and for a time it was all too easy to practice what I had learned. I had thought in those nascent days of my spiritual voyage I was perhaps rapidly becoming some kind of advanced spiritual master. Foolish self. I was but a small child in the faith, barely a toddler.

I don't remember the exact day in which I had to venture out from that heavenly place to be tested, the day the sugar-coating on the spiritual mint wore off and I had to taste the bitterness of the lack of consolation. But that time came, and I began walking through a valley which grew darker and harder by the step, and I did not persevere as I should have. So began my descent into a new void. My spiritual evening was falling, and the air grew frigid. A cold, dark night was descending, and it would be long.

CHAPTER 5

CHOICE

Thou hast created us for Thyself, and our heart is restless until it rests in Thee.

The Confessions, St. Augustine

The gleam of the setting sun reflected off the glass windows of the New York skyline and blinded me momentarily. I turned my head away from my window to the living world, and as the Hudson rushed up to meet us, I wondered what the bite of subfreezing air and icy water would feel like.

I thought about finding my BlackBerry and calling home, to leave a last message of farewell to my wife and children. I slid my briefcase out from under the seat in front of me – forgetting I had put the BlackBerry in my pocket – then reconsidered. There wasn't time, I thought to myself, and I didn't want the sounds of crash-landing in a plane to be my verbal legacy. So I started to slide my briefcase back under the seat, then recalled that I had placed the *Pietà* booklet in a side compartment. I quickly took the booklet out and slipped it into my shirt pocket, close to my heart.

Then a small epiphany occurred in my mind. I thought about the Chaplet of Mercy I had prayed the day before, and I recalled the words of Christ to Saint Faustina: Nothing would be refused if prayed in the three o'clock hour. I didn't have time to retrieve that booklet too – we were only seconds from the water – so I just thought about the image of Christ on the front cover. I could envision it very clearly: His hand held up in blessing, a slight gentle smile on His face, and the rays of light streaming from His heart.

"Where will you turn now?" The question came to me in my head. "Will you reconcile and trust? You must choose."

My conscience spoke to me, not in words but in very precise language – just clear pure thought instantaneously conveyed with no ambiguity and no trepidation.

In my mind, and with all the devotion and intensity I could muster, I said, "God, please be merciful to us, for the sake of your Son. Please spare us. I trust in you. Jesus, I trust in you. Blessed Mother of God, please pray for us." I then said the Lord's Prayer, a Hail Mary, and I looked out the window again, and we were below the skyline now, hurtling toward the river.

Just then I heard a man, another passenger, say, "Twenty seconds to impact!" How he could deduce that I didn't know, nor did I care. The flight attendants kept repeating, "Brace for impact, brace for impact! Put your heads down, put your heads down!" I watched others bend down; I looked back out the window. Other passengers called out to those in the exit rows, "Get ready on the doors, get ready to open the doors!" I saw a man half-stand, look back and nod. Then he sat down. I felt better that the passengers in the exit row were ready on the doors, however remote the likelihood of the plane staying together.

At that moment something happened to me that is hard to describe in words. I felt a surge of adrenaline course through my body, all my nerves seemed to prick up, and I felt a greater sense of awareness. Everything seemed to be stretching out, like time was slowing, and the lack of motion in the cabin and the strange peacefulness of our approach to the river made the world seem to halt suddenly. Something like a nudge on the doors of my conscience occurred, a firm thrust of gentle force pushing me to some conclusion. My mind felt agitated, as though I needed to do something, but what? We were about to crash into a freezing river, and my mind was telling me to *do something?* What?

The silent voice came to my soul and formed words in my conscience. The question – and the answer – manifested itself in my mind:

Will you accept My will for your life?

Then I knew and it became very clear: *I must choose now. That is all I have left to do. It may be the last decision of my earthly existence, but I must not shirk it. What is my decision? Will I? Can I accept the outcome whatever it may be, even if it means death?*

I knew that I needed to resolve whether I was willing to accept everything about my situation – that this was God's will for me this day, that I had chosen freely to go on this trip. I had to work through the conflict in my mind, whether this event would bring death or life, whether it would bring pain or joy, whether some would live and some would die, and I could do nothing to save others or myself. I needed to reconcile to the fact that I was not in control, and either in pride and anger turn away from God or in humility turn fully to Him and accept His will, however inscrutable it was and regardless of the consequences. The river was coming for me and I had to decide.

I knew not from where the question originated . . . was it God, my conscience? . . . and it did not matter. It was perfectly framed and waiting for my reply. Like the captain, who had to decide in a few moments where to glide a 73-ton jetliner in order to minimize loss of life, I had to make a decision on where to point my will and soul, and yield full control – yield it to the mysterious will of God. I closed my eyes and continued to envision the image of Jesus I had seen the day before on the Mercy booklet, and I prayed again, "Please be merciful to us. Please be merciful. . . . But it's okay . . . it's okay if it's your will I die today."

* * *

We were close enough to the water to make out the gently rolling currents. I thought of the people working in the buildings and driving in cars and how fortunate they were; the tranquillity of the river and the normality of the world seemed dreamlike in comparison to our predicament. It was so odd to know that physically I was perfectly fine as I sat there, but in just a few moments, I might be dead. If only we could somehow move out of the airplane and just get to the dry land, we would all be fine. So close to safety, and yet so very far.

Then I realized something had changed about my internal demeanor. The dark ethereal force that had been pulling my entire being downward into my seat like a surge of gravity was gone. A peaceful feeling came over me, along with the reconciliation of a multitude of conflicting emotions that swept through me and dissolved away. I looked around and saw passengers with their heads down, some holding hands. Faint cries from the stilled fuselage seemed to echo gently and fade away.

I reflected again on my family and children, how hard it would be for them. Yet, I could feel an enigmatic sense of calm surround me and support me. I was resigned yet somehow optimistic. One last decision to perhaps make in my life, and I knew I'd decided well. I hoped death would be quick and that I might at least know it was coming just before it hit. I thought of how merciful God had been in my life and how patient. He had prepared me for this over the past few months and weeks.

My renewed spiritual devotions, my visit to Saint Patrick Cathedral, the pensive mood I had been in since Christmas – it all made sense now. He was preparing me to meet Him and for that I was grateful, along with the time I had been given and the many blessings He had bestowed on me.

"Ten seconds!" the man shouted again, and I bowed my head, holding the left armrest and placing my right hand over my chest. With my fingers I felt the smooth side of the prayer booklet in my pocket, closed my eyes, and began quietly whispering the prayer to Saint Michael the Archangel. The journey was about to end, and I did not give up hope. The inner struggle was over.

CHAPTER 6

DARKNESS

I want to live in the spirit of faith. I accept everything that comes my way as given me by the loving will of God, who sincerely desires my happiness. And so I will accept with submission and gratitude everything that God sends me.

From the diary of St. Faustina

*A*fter the first two years of my conversion experience, my spiritual journey had become a battle, waged on the constantly shifting plains of my life. In the early part of my career I had been a workaholic, working into the evenings and on weekends. After Liz and I married and had children, although I did not keep as late hours, I continued to be consumed by work. The stress of it was always with me, and it affected my home life. I tended to internalize things, and I knew prayer helped, but I developed a tendency to rush prayer and I was unable to sustain a humble, wholehearted approach to my walk with God.

Still, from a career and monetary perspective, my life was good. Although my job was very demanding and often took me to the distant corners of the world, the business was performing well, and I was frequently promoted. It was the bull market of the new millennium, and I felt a certain sense of satisfaction from my business accomplishments. I had never considered myself overly ambitious, but in hindsight I can see that professional and financial success took over a more central part of my psyche than I would have cared to admit. I put all of my drive and mental faculties into my work, and it took all I had to give and kept demanding more.

Then, toward the end of 2003, things began to change, and not for the better. A few days before Christmas, our fifth child, a boy, was born almost forty-five days' premature with a very rare chromosome disorder that leads to multiple complications. Liz and I spent the next two weeks, over Christmas and New Year's, in the neonatal intensive care unit of our local hospital, hoping for some miracle that might allow him to live. But on Saturday, January 3, 2004, our fifth and last child, Aidan Michael Berretta, died in my arms.

During the following weeks, I struggled with a full range of emotions, including anger at God for my son's death. I knew it had to be harder still on Liz, who carried Aidan for eight months knowing he probably would not have much time. And yet I was grateful that we had him, even though his life was so short. He was part of our family, part of our lives, and I felt he somehow remained with us in spirit.

Then, within just two months, family crisis came once more. My father, who was 68 at the time, had not been feeling well for several months. When I returned home from a business trip one evening in March, my wife greeted me with the news that my Dad had been diagnosed with terminal, advanced pancreatic cancer. I felt as though I had been hit in the stomach with a baseball bat, and I just wanted to keel over and lie there on the floor. Dad was given at most a year to live, but he died just four months later, with me at his side.

Seeing him decline in health so rapidly, with brief intervals of relief following blood transfusions, was exhausting and depressing. Having watched my child and then my dad struggle to live, fighting for every breath, and being there with them both at the final moments, had a deep effect on me. I knew I needed to reassess my priorities. But at the same time, pressures at work were intensifying. My company, having just gone through a merger, needed me to do more. So I concentrated all of my energies on work, and whether as an escape or perhaps as an excuse, I allowed it to consume me.

Things seemed to get harder and harder. The challenges at work became intense and put even more strain on my home life. I felt God was placing too much on me, and I struggled to maintain my wavering faith. I really did not trust in God fully, even though I thought I did.

* * *

Uneasy and disillusioned, I started becoming inwardly reclusive again – my standard defensive tactic. Things just were not going my way, and I felt powerless to stop the downward spiral. The only escape from it all that I seemed to have was flying. Aware of my passion, Liz had given me a gift certificate for introductory flight lessons a few years earlier, and of course I had been instantly hooked.

I wound up purchasing the small Piper in which I had taken my first flying lesson, but quickly grew out of that, donated it to a charitable cause, and then bought a larger six-seat plane. It had taken me longer to obtain my pilot's license than was typical, partly by intention and partly by circumstance. By the time I passed my flight test, therefore, I was very competent. I mostly flew alone, and found it peaceful and satisfying. Flying a plane gave me a sense of being both free and in control. I finally was able to satisfy that latent dream I had developed so long ago as a boy, and for a while it was wonderful.

Of course, private aviation can be dangerous, and once while practicing takeoffs and landings one day in good weather, I had a near miss. Just after takeoff from the local municipal airport where I kept my plane, while pointing the nose down briefly so I could look ahead, I saw a Cessna 172 heading straight for me at the same altitude. The pilot hadn't bothered to communicate his whereabouts or approach to the airport. I immediately announced over the radio that I would commence a right turn, the evasive procedure generally used to avoid a midair collision. As I turned, I saw that the other plane continued to fly straight – on a collision course with my former heading. He never heeded my radio communications, and just continued about his business.

On another occasion, I experienced a second close call. While flying out of Charleston International Airport at night, I climbed to 6,500 feet on my way to 7,500, and then realized that I could go no higher. I leveled off, turned on the autopilot, and began checking gauges. Everything looked fine – oil temperature, oil pressure, fuel pressure, vacuum pump, voltmeter, and so forth. I was simply baffled. The engine had enough power to fly level, but not enough to climb further. I radioed Charleston approach and explained the situation. They asked if I was declaring an emergency; I said I was not, at least not yet. They were somewhat busy with other aircraft and gave me a vector to a small airport near Moncks Corner in South Carolina. Though I probably could have made it back to Charleston, I did not want to take any chances. I remembered the age-old aviator's adage: "There are old pilots and there are bold pilots, but there are no old, bold pilots." And I also thought about the other saying: "It is better to be on the ground wishing you were in the air, than in the air wishing you were on the ground."

Air traffic control indicated I was right over the small airport, but the runway lights were directly beneath me and the wings of my plane blocked my view of them. I began a slow, turning descent, and I watched my altimeter bleed down as I circled to try and locate the airport. Two thousand, one thousand five hundred, one thousand. I knew that if I could not locate the runway soon, the situation would become precarious very quickly. I would probably end up clipping trees and crashing into the dark fields.

Knowing I was directly over the runway, I decided to extend my turn out a little, hoping I could catch the threshold lights or the beacon. For some reason I recalled a line from the movie *Spirit of St. Louis*, in which Jimmy Stewart played the part of Charles Lindbergh, the first pilot to make a successful transatlantic crossing from New York to Paris. He was exhausted from his thirty-three-hour flight after dealing with icing, fog, and other trying circumstances, and on approach to Paris, at the point of collapse, he prayed, "Oh, God, help me." I repeated that simple prayer in the back of my mind as I maneuvered in an attempt to find the airport. Finally, at two hundred feet above ground level, I saw the runway lights shining dimly. I made an abrupt left downwind approach, quickly turned base to final, and then dropped down about midway down the runway, stopping just short of the other end by no more than fifty feet. The whole time I had remained calm, as I was trained to, but once on the ground I became aware that I was sweating and shaking slightly. But I had made it.

It turned out that the engine in my plane had lost a cylinder shortly after takeoff, with no indication. Once again I had been fortunate, and as with the previous incident, I perhaps did not take the whole episode seriously enough.

* * *

As 2006 approached, the economy continued to boom, and the business I managed was having its best year of growth in its history. I had never been on a cruise and always had wanted to go on one, so I decided to take my family on a transatlantic crossing from New York to England on the *Queen Mary 2*.

A few days into our voyage, the captain made an interesting announcement. He told us we were sailing almost directly above the location where the *Titanic* had sunk. The thought made me contemplate the fate of the passengers on that infamous voyage, and as I walked the decks that cold, windy night, I felt great sorrow for what they must have endured. I could not imagine their plight: many dying of hypothermia within minutes after sinking, others going down with the ship and resigned to their destiny, and still others clinging to life in small boats, awaiting rescue.

As my family and I dined the next evening, I remember feeling a particular thoughtfulness and gratitude for my life, notwithstanding its trials. My investments had performed well, and I recall thinking about the possibility of early retirement if things continued on their track.

The cruise was relaxing, and the week in England afterward was serene and peaceful, but returning to work was like falling into that freezing ocean we had just crossed. My inbox was bursting with emails full of bad news. The initial domino had fallen in the capital markets, with the meltdown of short-term securities backed by subprime collateral. Within a few short months, more dominoes fell, one after the other. I saw the asset management business I had helped build and lead for so many years begin to unwind in a few weeks, even though no part of it had been involved in creation of subprime mortgage collateral. We were simply one of the many victims of the global economic slide. I had no idea – and there were few economists who did either – that the genesis of the subprime disaster would lead to a global credit crisis the likes of which had not been seen since the Great Depression.

By the time the final domino tumbled in the autumn of 2008, I like many Americans found myself a much poorer man. Much of the equity in my home was lost, and my retirement accounts had declined significantly. Stock options I owned, once worth a small fortune to me, had become valueless. Yet I was more fortunate than the many thousands who were losing their jobs, as the economy, which had enjoyed the most aggressive bull run in American history, struck a black iceberg and was fast sinking.

In the midst of all the din of worry, fear, and media hype of the moment-by-moment drama, a still small voice began ringing in my ears. Whether I received some new grace, or whether God had used suffering, death, and financial collapse to humble me and make me more receptive to his promptings, I don't know. But I was determined to be attentive to that voice; to reorder my priorities and reclaim the zeal I had lost. So I made a New Year's resolution to improve my spiritual life, to deepen my commitment to my faith and my relationship with God.

I read about a woman who prayed the Rosary for nearly twelve hours straight while hiding under a hotel bed in Mumbai, as terrorists walked the halls stalking guests and searching for people to kill. She and her husband miraculously survived that ordeal, and I recalled the promises of the Rosary that I had learned about long ago. This testimony inspired me, and I began dusting off those old pious devotions I had partially abandoned, praying the Rosary every day and trying my best to meditate on the gospel scenes with attention, humility, and commitment.

By the time January 2009 arrived, something felt different for me in the new year. It was something I could not quite pinpoint – something that made me pensive and reflective. I saw with new clarity that I had been too attached to the material things in my life, too reliant on the transient security they seemed to offer, and too inclined to believe that I was in control of my life.

This realization inspired me further to become more disciplined in daily prayer. I thought about all the time, effort, and sacrifice I had put into my career, at times at the expense of my family life, and how little it was now worth. I was not sorry that I had worked hard, understand – just that I had made it too much the centerpiece of my mind, my time, and my life.

* * *

On Monday, January 12, I arrived home from work in the late evening and sat down to eat my dinner. My kids were finishing up homework and readying for bed, so I turned on the television to catch the news. I watched for a few minutes: it was the same gloomy economic talk, juxtaposed against the upcoming presidential inauguration. I decided to flip over to the Catholic channel, EWTN, to find a program that might be more uplifting.

Just getting underway was a biography about a German Redemptorist priest named Father Francis Xavier Seelos, who came to the United States in 1843 to minister to German immigrants. In conjunction with my New Year resolution, I had been thinking about how to create a simple routine for my daily prayer life that would help me stay focused and disciplined. The biography on Father Seelos portrayed him as a very practical and humble man who might have some answers. After the program ended, I kissed my kids goodnight and got on the computer, where I found a website dedicated to Father Seelos that offered a ten-step guide he had espoused, perfect for my life as a married man and father. After a few minutes of reading I also came across a quote that stuck in my mind:

"It is not your justice but God's mercy which is the motive of your trust. He is the God of all consolations and the Father of mercies. He does not wish the death of sinners but that they be converted and live."

Father Seelos's focus on the mercy of God impressed me. It had been many years since I had dwelled on His mercy. Instead I had formed in my mind the image of a God who had become frustrated with me: for my lack of advancement in the spiritual life, for my inconstant inner fidelity. But as Father Seelos reminded me in another passage, "The assistance of power from above is plainly visible, so that we are often humbled at seeing the great mercy and goodness of God!"

I realized I had been too hard on myself, and then allowed discouragement to dissuade me even more. It is an easy trap in the spiritual life. Lack of perseverance leads to mistakes and laxity, and that leads to discouragement, which stalls the flight of the soul. Just as every pilot learns in training how to avoid the dreaded death spiral, so every Christian must return, when his spiritual engines are damaged after takeoff, to a trusting reliance on God's infinite mercy. Father Seelos's words were to be for me not only edifying but, in just a few days, prophetic.

CHAPTER 7

IMPACT

It was, for him, as though the rock were a giant hard door into another world. A burst of fear and shock and black as he hit, and then he was adrift.

From *Jonathan Livingston Seagull*, by Richard Bach

*T*he sleek plane hit the water.

It felt much harder than I expected: like landing on concrete with the gear up and nothing to absorb the impact. My head hit the seat in front of me twice, and it was hard, but I felt no pain even though it cut my head. There was a sound like an explosion of water, the plane shook violently back and forth, and at any second I thought death would come. Would it be from the fuselage splitting apart and water hitting us at a hundred and forty miles an hour? Would we cartwheel across the river and all be thrown out of the plane, dying instantly or drowning within seconds? My senses strained to feel whatever was coming, as if I could somehow prepare for it and defend myself.

Then, amid what sounded like a rushing waterfall, I felt

gravity pulling us hard to the right as the back of the plane slewed counterclockwise like some amusement park ride. As we slid, I felt this was it at last. These were finally the culminating moments. We were about to roll over and break up. I thought that at any instant I would be killed or thrown into unconsciousness.

Suddenly the turning stopped, and the splashing sound of water slowly subsided. The plane rocked a little, and I looked up and was simply astonished at what I saw. We were floating, with the nose pointing out of the water slightly, and the fuselage was fully intact!

Once over the shock of still being alive and seeing the plane floating, seemingly in one piece, I looked at the man to my right and said, "We can do this! We can get through this!" He acknowledged my optimism with an affirmative nod of his head and then looked down the aisle. Passengers began shouting to each other, "Go! Go!" and "Move it now!"

Within a few seconds after the plane stabilized itself in the water, passengers started standing up, grabbing their seat cushions, and making their way into the aisle. A few passengers impulsively went for their luggage, but others exclaimed, "Leave them! Just go!"

When my turn came to get up and enter the aisle, I tried to sit up and realized my seatbelt was still fastened. I quickly grabbed the metal clip and unbuckled, knowing that precious seconds were being wasted in the process. I reached under the seat to try to clutch the life vest. I could feel it in my hands but couldn't get a good enough grip on it. I had to stand up and go. My turn had come, and I did not want to hold others up. I needed to move fast, and once I stood up and looked down the aisle, my mind was focused on how quickly we might be sinking, so I didn't think to reach back down and grab the seat cushion. By that time I was in the aisle, part of the mass of humanity slowly making its way to the exit doors.

As we walked on to the doors, there were some shouts and cries, but for the most part things were orderly. I looked down to my right and saw one woman sitting alone, motionless and stunned. I stopped and told her to get moving, and she sat up and joined the shocked brigade. As I neared the left exit door, I assumed that I would be in the water swimming, and unlike most passengers I saw, I had no seat cushion or life vest. I felt I could swim for perhaps twenty minutes or so, but I knew the cold waters would not allow for much longer.

As I reached the exit doors, most of the passengers who had sat in the rows forward of the wings had already evacuated. I knew there was no turning back to get to my seat. So I walked forward and began looking down into each row, hoping there might be an extra cushion. All I saw were empty seat frames and the carpet beneath them. Then, just as I was about to abandon the search, I spotted one cushion lying at an angle on the seat frame, four or five rows up. I picked it up and made my way back to the exit doors on the left side.

My mind moved at warp speed trying to predict what was to come. What would the water feel like? How long can I survive in it? The women, children, and elderly will be rescued first, and they should be, but it will be slow and we will all be in freezing waters. How long can I survive this? Can I swim for it? Will I have to swim to shore?

Do you still trust?

How fast will the plane sink? It is already sinking. Move to the doors. One step at a time. Move out of the plane and go to the water. Must not make a mistake. Must help others if possible. Go out. Then figure it out from there. You have survived this much. It is incredible that the plane stayed together. You can do this! We can do this!

What is your faith made of now?

As I bent down a little to make it through the doorway, I fully expected to be in the water, holding onto my seat cushion. There was nothing in my experience or even in my imagination that prepared me for what I saw next.

* * *

When I tilted my head up and emerged blinking through the door, there were passengers walking down the wing, their feet fully submerged in the water. I had to kneel initially as I got onto the wing, to ensure that I didn't slip, and I kept one hand on the fuselage. I moved to the right and stood on the corner of the wing, just where it connected to the plane. I braced myself there, and turned to lend a hand to passengers who were coming out of that particular door. Another man stood to my left doing the same.

We looked across the river in both directions, trying to gauge the distance. "How far do you think it is?" I asked him. "Too far," he replied. The currents were strong, and we could see the skyline passing by. We both concluded there was no way to swim for it. Even if the currents did not drown us, the icy waters surely would be our death. "Come on boats, come on helicopters!" I just said aloud, knowing that they would come – just not how long or how many.

I then glanced toward the front of the plane and saw inflated shoots extending from the exit doors, floating like rafts. The one on the left front of the plane had passengers on it, but it did not look full. I leaned my head back into the exit door to see if there was another raft on the other side of the plane. A flight attendant was walking down the aisle, continuing to instruct passengers to exit onto the wing. I looked at her and asked if there was room on the rafts and whether there was one on the right side too. She answered yes to both questions. As passengers were still filing on our wing, I told them to go forward and get on the rafts, as the wing was getting crowded, methodically drifting down into the water. A few passengers moved on to the front, and others kept climbing onto the wing.

There appeared to be a few passengers in the water swimming, and I could tell they were heading for the wing or the rafts. It wasn't clear whether they had instinctively jumped into the river or had accidentally fallen off the wing. As they approached, other passengers helped them get on the wing, risking their own stable place on it to help those desperately trying to get out of the freezing water.

As I stood there, I felt euphoric that we had all apparently survived the crash landing and that the plane had stayed together, floating long enough for us to get outside. I figured, as I am sure many others did as well, that a few boats would come, and perhaps a helicopter or two. But I also guessed that the plane would sink faster and faster as the back of the fuselage gradually filled with water. I looked at the seat cushion in my hands, and examined the two straps on the back of it. I thought it might help me stay afloat, but would I be able to swim with it? I wanted to be as mobile as possible. I saw other passengers donning life vests and realized it would be prudent to have one too, so I waited for the exit door to clear and then headed back into the plane.

There were still a few passengers in the aisle to the right, making their way to the exit doors on the other side. Going back to my seat was not an option. I looked left, and just in front of the flight deck was a crew member. I thought that was my best option: perhaps there were more life vests stored somewhere up there.

As I turned left, I saw an elderly woman struggling to walk, with another female passenger behind her, helping her. I walked up behind them and tried to keep them and myself calm as we crept along to the front of the plane.

We reached the galley way, where a crew member helped the two women onto the raft off the right door. I asked if there was an extra life vest and was given one, from where I do not know. I stood just inside the plane by the right door and looked over the vest to find the straps. They were slightly intertwined, and my hands, which had been in the water briefly, then in the frigid air, were by now numb and shaking slightly. At that moment another crew member, who had been standing to my right and watching me struggle, took the vest from me and untangled the strap, then gave me brief instructions on how to put it on. As he did so, he kept looking down the aisle, checking to see how things were proceeding with the evacuation. I did not realize at the time that this man was the captain, Chesley Sullenberger, but his cool and friendly demeanor instantly encouraged me. I realized he was one of the pilots, and I thanked him for helping me and saving us, then made my way out the door.

As I slid down the shoot, which effectively functioned as a raft, I could feel the cold penetrate me, and my right hand in particular was trembling. The raft was crowded, and I worried that some passengers might panic and we would tip over. I tried to keep myself calm. Like most of us, I assumed the plane would be completely submerged any moment. The passengers on the right wing were about waist deep in the water by then. Many held hands and huddled close together to keep warm and help each other any way they could. I could see they were all looking to the right, some shouting and some stone-faced.

I then saw the object of their fascination: a large ferryboat, slowing as it approached the wing. It was an incredible relief to see help on the way, and I was glad it was headed for that wing. Those passengers desperately needed to be saved first, as the plane continued slowly making its way down.

Passengers in our raft kept shifting around, some trying to stand, others waving. I looked back to the door of the plane, then back to the ferryboat. The left side of the aircraft was completely obscured by the fuselage, so I could not tell if boats had arrived there or not. Then I felt a surge of wind blow down on us, and the familiar sound of a helicopter rotor. The copter flew in a semicircle just behind the tail of the plane, and I watched to see if it held rescue divers.

The plane kept gently sinking, and although the rescue of the passengers on the right wing was proceeding, it seemed slow. Each passenger had to walk to a certain area on the wing and try to grab onto the rails of the ladder in the bow of the ferryboat. It was agonizing to watch them try to anticipate the exact right time to go for the ladder, and many went into the water instead. But they all helped each other, one at a time, waiting their turn to reach for safety and return to the world again.

* * *

I glanced back down into the water, and froze with a new strain of fear. I could see that there were two cords tethering our raft to the plane. I had no idea how long the rescue would take for the passengers on the wing, but I realized that when the plane finally went down it would take our life raft with it, leaving us all to fight for our lives in the frigid current. I simply could not believe that, having come this far, we now faced what seemed to be an unavoidable outcome.

My instinct was to grab the cords, so I went for the left one. I pulled with my left hand as I steadied myself on the raft with my right. It took effort, but the cord pulled free after a few seconds. I then switched hand positions, and grabbed the right cord with my right hand. It didn't budge, even though I pulled with everything I had. The man sitting behind me to my right saw me struggling, and he grabbed the cord too, and we both pulled together. The moment felt desperate to us, the last battle to wage in this bizarre ordeal of fear, and it seemed silly and unfair.

The downwash of the helicopter rotors was right over us again, and the wind felt like knives piercing through my body.

The other man and I realized it was futile to try to free the remaining tether. I looked at him and said, "Can you believe this? We've come this far, and now we're just going to all be in the river."

As we looked back toward the ferryboat off the right wing, we saw another up from behind the plane, turning hard left and slowing quickly. It approached the wing, and as it did, the first ferryboat pulled back and then turned toward us. It was a perfect maneuver, saving precious minutes in the process by keeping the second boat from having to go around and make a wider loop back. The ferryboat approached, and we tried to sit motionless, just waiting, fearing if we stood up, the raft might flip over. The bow grew large in our view and came at us at an angle, and its wake rocked the raft.

I looked back at the tether, and the thought came to me: *we need to find something to cut it.* I shouted to the few men who stood on the deck at the bow, as they began throwing life preservers to us, some landing on the raft, others going into the water. "We need a knife! We need a knife! Can you find a knife or something to cut?" The man who had worked with me on the tether yelled out too, but the men on deck looked at us baffled.

Finally, one of them realized our predicament, and there was a discussion among them. One approached the rail of the bow and looked at me, holding a pocketknife in his hand. I knelt down in the raft and looked right at him. He slowly made the pitch and I focused with my entire mind to make the catch. The knife met my hands and I clutched it firmly. Got it! But my hands were so cold and numb, from being in the water and fighting the tether, that I could not make my fingers work to open the blade. I gave it to another passenger, and he opened it and handed it back. I cut the tether, almost leaning too far but held fast by the other man, and we were finally free of the plane. I handed the knife over, as I could not close it. An open knife on an inflatable raft is not a great combination, so he tossed it back on the deck.

The ferryboat, now gently bumping our raft, was ready for us. The ladder, with two thick silver rails on each side, was within reach. A woman nearest to the ladder got up first, helped by two men standing near her. It was an arduous process that seemed to be happening in slow motion, painfully methodical. Each time a passenger would exit onto the ladder, the raft pushed away from the bow of the boat.

At the end of the raft closest to the boat, I kept reaching to try to grab onto the rails of the ladder and hold the raft in place. But it was futile, as the waves were bobbing all of us up and down, and the progress continued to be slow. I looked up, and a man on the ferryboat deck, several feet above me, must have read my mind, for without speaking he lowered the loop end of a very thick rope, which I put my right arm through and held tight with my hand. We both had had the same idea simultaneously: I would hold one end, and he would hold the other, stabilizing the raft and keeping it as close as possible to the ferryboat.

He shouted down to me, "Can you tie it to the raft?"

I just shook my head. There was no edge or anything to hold the rope fast, so I knew the only option was to stand there holding it with my right arm.

Just then, the elderly lady who'd had trouble exiting the plane made her way to the edge of the raft, but she was struggling. Since she was unable to lift herself onto the ladder, three men put another large rope around her waist, and then began hoisting her up slowly. I could tell she was holding onto the rails as hard as she could, straining to use any last vestige of strength left in her arms and legs. She made it to the top, disappeared over the edge of the deck, and we all gave a cheer of relief.

As the women exited one by one, we made a makeshift stairway out of the seat cushions so the step up onto the edge of the raft was less precarious. We all worried that someone might fall just as they left the raft and leaped forward to the ladder.

By this point, my right hand was almost completely numb, and I kept shaking it to keep the blood moving. Passengers carefully made their way onto the ferryboat ladder and climbed to freedom. It seemed to take so long, watching them one by one, and I eagerly anticipated my turn.

Finally a tall man, the last one on the raft except for me, looked at me and gestured to go ahead. I nodded and just said, "I'm fine, I wanna keep the raft tight." I was worried that if I let go of the rope, we might push back from the ferryboat. He went up the ladder and disappeared.

I slid the looped rope off my right arm, and grabbed onto the rails. Not wanting to be too hasty and risk slipping, I made sure my footing was secure on each rung. Step by step I climbed, shivering all the way up. As my eyesight cleared the top rung, I looked up and saw two men, each with an arm outstretched toward me. I looked down at my feet to see if they were making their way squarely on the steps so I would not slip. As I reached the top of the ladder and moved forward onto the deck, the men half hugged me, patting me on the back as I walked by them. My eyes welled up for the first time, and I fought off the tears. They said, "Great job! You're okay, you made it, you made it, you've all made it!"

When I walked into the open doors of the ferryboat cabin, the warmth of the interior air felt as though I was stepping into room lit by a giant fireplace. The air enveloped me, and I took off my life vest and dropped it on the floor. I saw a passenger kneel down, and another crying. People were hugging each other; others were dialing on cell phones. I paced back and forth and tried to get warm all over, hoping my feet and hands were not frostbitten. My mind kept telling me, "I am alive! I made it! I think we all made it!" That last thought provided the greatest euphoria I had ever experienced in my life.

CHAPTER 8

LIFE

For death begins with life's first breath, and life begins at touch of death.

John Oxenham, twentieth-century
English poet and journalist

WOLF BLITZER, CNN Anchor: We're going to continue to stay on this breaking news story right here in "The Situation Room." A U.S. Airways plane – you see it right there – it's in the Hudson River. It's an Airbus A-320, one hundred thirty-five people, we're told, on board. This is U.S. Airways Flight 1549 from LaGuardia in New York City, scheduled to go to Charlotte, North Carolina. And we're told, shortly after takeoff, it went into the Hudson River, which is not very far away, as you know, from LaGuardia Airport. This is right off of Manhattan.

We have no indications of injuries or anything along those lines, although, if you take a look at the pictures, you see lots of boats already and ferries all around that plane. You can see much of the plane still above the water, but some of it beginning to go underneath. We don't know how deep that water is in the Hudson River right there. All right, there you see it, the plane right in the middle of your screen. And you see those boats, those ferries right around it. We're told by the Coast Guard, according to our own Homeland Security correspondent, Jeanne Meserve, that life vests have been thrown into the Hudson River in case folks are trying to get out of that plane. It's very cold in New York, in the twenties right now, and the temperature of that water in the Hudson River only in the forties. And even as we're watching what is going on, you see more vessels heading toward that U.S. Airways A-320 aircraft that was on the way from New York to LaGuardia.

Peter Goelz, a former managing director of the National Transportation Safety Board, is joining us on the phone right now. You know, it was only the other day we were saying, Peter, there hadn't been a major airline disaster over the past two years. Then, a lot, we see this. But take a look at; take a look at these pictures. You see that tail drifting over there, Peter.

PETER GOELZ: Extraordinary. I was at a luncheon yesterday, where the secretary of transportation was touting that record. And I remember a number of us up at the table knocking on wood. I guess it didn't work. This is just extraordinary, Wolf.

BLITZER: What's the procedure for evacuating those? We're told one hundred thirty-five people aboard that plane in the – in the Hudson River right now? How does that work? Because it looks like that aircraft, if you watched it a few moments ago, was higher up in the water than it is right now.

GOELZ: Yes, it's no question. As I have been watching it, it's sinking lower. In this case, the over-the-wings exits would be the ones to use. And, you know, those are obscured right now.

BLITZER: So, how do these people get out of that plane?

GOELZ: That's going to be the challenge. They have got to get out over the wing. And if the front or the rear doors are open, they're . . . they're at least partially underwater.

BLITZER: Is it possible to open up the . . . let's say the front of the plane door, if the . . . or both of those doors in the front of the plane, because it looks higher in the front, obviously, than it does near the tail in the back. Is it possible to open those doors if they are partially submerged?

GOELZ: You can get them open, but it's more of a challenge.

BLITZER: Because then the water starts rushing in?

GOELZ: That's exactly right.

BLITZER: So, under a circumstance like this, the flight attendants, the pilot, the co-pilot, what are they trained to do?

GOELZ: Well, they are trained to get these doors open, but it's awfully difficult to train for a situation like this. The majority of the training is for on-the-ground accidents. And when you have got a plane that's now even deeper submerged than it was just five minutes ago, there are some real challenges. We can only pray that a bunch of these passengers got out right away, before the plane started to really take on water.

* * *

As I rubbed my arms and legs to try to get warm, I felt for my BlackBerry in my left pocket. I had completely forgotten it was there, and in my state of shock, I had not even noticed it. I wondered if it was still working, and when I turned it on, it came to life like nothing had happened. At that instant I saw a call coming through from my assistant. She and hundreds of thousands of others had heard the news and were watching the plane on television, as it floated down the Hudson River.

I then began dialing for home, as I checked my watch to see the time. It was 3:47, and I knew my wife would be leaving to pick up my two older sons, Jonathan and Evan, at the bus stop. The voicemail came on, and I left a short message. I then dialed her cell phone, assuming she must have her radio on, as she often listened to the news in her car.

She answered, and I blurted out, "I'm okay, I'm okay! Glad I got you!"

She replied, somewhat nonplussed, "That's nice to hear . . . I'm okay too."

I then realized my mistaken assumption. I took a deep breath and said, "I'm sorry, I've just gotten out of the Hudson River; our plane crashed and I was on the wing and now I'm on a boat, but I'm fine. I think everyone made it. It must be all over the news, so call me when you get home."

Liz knew of my occasional tendency to jest, and must for a moment have thought I was joking. But then she could tell by my tone that I was indeed serious, however farfetched the story sounded.

"Oh my gosh, are you all right? I can't believe it!" she exclaimed.

"I'm fine, just very cold. Turn on the news when you get home, and I'll call you as soon as I can and know more about what happened. I love you."

We were just reaching the pier, and I could hear the sound of the ferryboat engines going into reverse. We docked, and then all filed into the terminal area. There were already police, medics, and other personnel waiting for us. I began to pace around, trying to regain some feeling of life in my feet and hands. As I walked from the ferryboat into the terminal area, my cell rang again, and I saw it was a call from the work colleague whom I had spoken to just prior to boarding the flight. I said, "Hey, Joe, are you calling to tell me my plane just crashed?" He said, "Yes, I am, very glad you're all right." We both half-chuckled, and it felt good to find a moment of levity in the unbelievably intense time that had just passed.

More officials came into the terminal area, and they began counting the passengers. It seemed that about sixty passengers had been brought to our terminal, and I learned that there were three other areas where other passengers had been taken. A coffee station had been set up, and I made my way over to get a cup. As I began to take a sip, a policeman approached and asked for my name. He asked if I needed warm clothes, and I saw a box nearby with sweatshirts and pants. I put on one of the dark blue sweatshirts, thanked him, and he went on to another passenger.

* * *

BLITZER: Soledad O'Brien is on the scene for us in New York. Soledad, what are you seeing? What are you hearing?

SOLEDAD O'BRIEN, CNN Special Correspondent: Yes, mostly, what I can see is the tail of this plane. And it is surrounded by ferries and smaller boats, Coast Guard and police vessels. They have really been shooing the hundreds of people who have come out to line the – the pathway along the water (inaudible) Twelfth Street in Manhattan to get a better look, and some of them saying, "Hey, is that a plane in the water?" because we are incredibly close to where it has actually landed in the water. It's drifting or being pulled – it's hard to really tell, because it's surrounded by ferries – very, very quickly. I mean, for me to keep up, I actually have to walk at – at quite a clip. And the police officers have set up a perimeter right near this big sports arena, because what they're going to do is bring some of the injured folks in there. And they have been trying to clear all the pedestrians and every-body who is just sitting around watching, getting them out of the way. And, really, Twelfth Street, for blocks and blocks and blocks, is now just absolutely full of ambulances.

BLITZER: It's taking on water and it's going down. But we're told, at least according to two passengers who survived, they believe everyone on board managed to escape either the front exits, the rear exits, or those emergency exits over the wings and get on some of those boats that quickly hurried over to the scene and take them to safety, which is very good news, because if there were more people on board, they would be in deep trouble right now if they couldn't get those doors open. But that plane is going down even as we speak, but we hope and believe that everyone on board is off and safe. The plane went down in the Hudson River, near, we're told – the passengers are near Forty-second Street. Is that the closest sort of cross street where you are right now?

O'BRIEN: You know, I'm headed way past Forty-second Street. I am way down south of Twenty-third Street, which is where I started, and I probably walked another ten or twelve blocks south since I hopped on the phone, because it is really moving fast. And again, all I can see now is the tip of the tail. It's not very far off land, as you can probably tell from the pictures, but it's moving at a clip of several blocks a minute, frankly. And it has – at first, the report that I was hearing, it was at Fiftieth Street. Then I looked out the window and I could see it at Twenty-third Street, and so I ran out to take a look.

BLITZER: Chad Myers is on the scene – he's not on the scene, but knows what's going on in terms of the very cold air and water temperature in the Hudson River area – Chad.

CHAD MYERS, CNN Meteorologist: Yes, that water very, very close to thirty-two degrees. There's a buoy that is just down from Lady Liberty. It has about forty-degree water there, but that's mixing in with a little bit of ocean water. Where this plane originally landed, on up around Fiftieth Street, certainly no ocean water was coming in there.

So we know that this is the water literally coming out of the Adirondacks, straight down from Albany, barely liquid, at thirty-two point five. Wolf, I also have a picture of what happened to the plane. It left LaGuardia at Runway Four, turned to the north, and headed on up – a typical departure. Turned to the left. I don't know where in this place we did have that explosion. They said it actually exploded – the noise was heard before the big turn, the big turn down the Hudson River. And right there, this was the last ping we got from the plane. It was at 300 feet in the sky doing one hundred fifty-three knots. The next ping that we would have received, the plane was in the water, and it was floating downriver. The reason why I think the plane is losing a lot of elevation now, is sinking, is because the authorities have opened up the front doors. Those front doors are allowing the water to pour in from the rear doors that are already open. For a while, with the front doors remaining closed, there was just an air bubble inside. That air bubble was keeping that plane afloat. Still think probably the way that plane went down in such a very slight angle, witnesses say that he really just eased the plane into the water. The bottom of the plane did not come apart, and so that compartment below that would be holding the luggage, holding other things, still full of air. That's why the plane didn't go down in a big hurry. Because the plane didn't break up, all of these people are alive to tell the story – Wolf.

BLITZER: It's an amazing story.

* * *

As I walked around, trying to process everything that had happened, the feeling of elation at being alive encompassed my whole being. I was in awe of the incredible skill the captain had shown in landing in the river safely. I wanted to thank him and hoped that he and the crew had been brought to our terminal, so I began looking for them. Sure enough, I found them speaking with officials, and I walked up and spoke first with the co-pilot, Jeff Skiles. I shook his hand and thanked him, and told him he was a hero. He pointed to the captain and just said, "He did it all." I knew that was not entirely true, and I respected his humility.

I then approached the captain and reached out for his hand, saying, "You saved us all. You are a true hero! Thank you, thank you." He had his coat and cap on, looking as though he had just finished a morning cup of coffee and was headed out for the office. He was calm, and his countenance was mild and controlled. He just sort of nodded his head in gratitude for my remarks, looked me in the eyes, and shook my hand.

Two of the flight attendants were also sitting nearby. I thanked them both for their courage and professionalism; they seemed a little shaken, but calm (if a bit teary-eyed). I hugged them and then made my way back for more coffee.

After refilling my cup, I checked my watch and thought that by now my family would be home by then, watching the news. Then a dark-haired man approached me, and politely asked if I was a passenger. I replied that I was. He shook my hand and introduced himself as Adam Reiss with CNN, and asked if I would be willing to speak with Wolf Blitzer, one of the world's most recognized names in TV journalism. I just stood there, trying to assimilate his words; I was still in such a state of shock that I couldn't quite connect the dots. Wolf Blitzer, Wolf Blitzer. It finally hit me – *okay, I remember now.*

I agreed to what I imagined would be me just having a one-on-one conversation with Wolf. Once I was connected to the control room at CNN on my BlackBerry, however, I realized it would not be a private conversation. I looked at Adam, and he said it was going to be aired live. The control room contact asked if I could hear him and indicated thirty seconds before we were live. I thought to myself, *Well, the last countdown I*

US Airways Flight 1549 descends into the Hudson River. (AP Photo/Trela Media)

Airline passengers line the wings of the Airbus A-320 jetliner awaiting rescue. (AP Photo/Steven Day)

The first boat arrives to rescue passengers from the wings of the US Airways Airbus A-320 jetliner (AP Photo/Steven Day)

Boats approach to rescue the airline passengers off of the wings of the US Airways Airbus A-320 jetliner. (AP Photo/Steven Day)

The last passengers move away from the sinking Airbus A-320 US Airways in an inflatable raft (AP Photo/Bebeto Matthews)

With all of the passengers rescued, the jetliner sinks further into the Hudson River. (Photo by Edouard H.R. Glucl-Pool/Getty Images)

Rescue boats float near the plane. (Photo by Neilson Barnard/Getty Images)

The statue of liberty stands in the background as rescue boats float next to the plane. (Photo by Chris McGrath/Getty Images)

The wreckage of US Airways flight 1549 floats in the Hudson River near Battery Park City in New York City. (Photo by Mario Tama/Getty Images)

A crane is positioned over the submerged wreckage of US Airways flight 1549 as it prepares to lift the Airbus A-320 from its makeshift mooring along a seawall in lower Manhattan. (Photo by Edouard H.R. Glucl-Pool/ Getty Images)

U.S. Airways Airbus A-320 is seen on a barge in the Hudson River Saturday January 17, 2009 in New York City. (Photo by Daniel Barry/Getty Images)

One of the engines from US Airways Flight 1549 is lifted up from the Hudson River on January 23, 2009 in New York City. The other engine was still attached to the plane when it was removed from the Hudson the week before. (Photo by Daniel Bary/Getty Images)

Workers walk past one of the engines of the U.S. Airways Airbus A-320 January 17, 2009 in New York City. (Photo by Daniel Barry/Getty Images)

Rescue Workers of US Airways Flight 1549 attend the ringing of the NASDAQ opening bell in Times Square on January 20, 2009 in New York City.

Me, at age 3, with my family in Fort Lauderdale, FL. Back, left to right, my mother Charlotte, my sister, Michelle, my paternal grandmother Rosa. Front, left to right, me, my sister Tina.

Me, in the 6th grade. My first year in a Catholic school.

Me, as a freshman in college.

Me, as a sophomore in college with some of my family. Back, left to right, my brother-in-law Bob (Michelle), my father Frederick Sr., me. Front, left to right, my brother-in-law Mike, my sister Tina and her baby Shannon.

My wife, Liz, and I on our wedding day.

Me, with my parents and siblings. My father Frederick, my sister Tina, my sister Michelle, me, my mother Charlotte. This was the first time we were all together since my parents' divorce.

My immediate family. Back, left to right: my son Jonathan, my wife Liz, me. Front, left to right: my son Benjamin, my daughter Lauren, my son Evan.

My father and I in Orvieto, Italy. This was the last picture of us together before my father's death in July, 2004.

Me, next to my first plane, a single-engine Piper Warrior, the plane in which I learned to fly.

heard was just prior to surviving a plane crash in a river. I some-
how survived that, so I guess I can survive this.

BLITZER: Adam, do you have another passenger there with you who survived this crash?

REISS: I do, Wolf. Before I give you Fred Berretta, I want to just sort of paint a picture for you here in the rescue area. Most of the people here are draped in blankets, shivering, obviously very, very relieved, Wolf, just an incredible experience they just went through. There's a lot of hugs. We're still seeing people come in out from the water. I just saw one gentleman without a shirt. And I saw another gentleman with some blood on his shirt. But everybody seems to be in pretty good shape, just grateful to be alive. And now I'm going to put you on with Fred Berretta. He was also on the flight.

BLITZER: All right, Fred, this is . . .

BERRETTA: Hi, Wolf.

BLITZER: This is Wolf Blitzer. I'm . . . I'm really thrilled that you and your fellow passengers managed to escape this U.S. Airways plane that made this emergency landing in the Hudson River. Apparently, we're being told preliminary . . . preliminary information, according to the FAA, says it looks like a bird strike, meaning either a bird or a flock of birds, hit the jet engines. What did it feel like? Tell us what was going on from your perspective. First of all, where in the plane were you sitting?

BERRETTA: Wolf, I was in seat 16-A, which was right actually over the engine that was flaming. And we were still on the ascent. And the engine blew out. And then the pilot turned around, made a . . , made a line for the . . . the river. There was just a lot of silence. And, obviously, everyone was just waiting to hear what the pilot would say. And a few moments went by, and he just said, "Prepare for impact." And then we went into the water. And I have got to tell you, I have flown in a lot of planes. That was a phenomenal landing on the part of the pilots. I really want to thank them. And, by the grace of God, I think . . . I think everyone made it off the plane.

BLITZER: Well, that's what we're hearing. Your fellow passenger, Alberto Panero, was just on with us. All right, Fred, so, walk us through exactly what happened from the time of impact to, when this U.S. Airways jetliner landed in the Hudson River, and the time you managed to get out of your seats and then get to an exit.

BERRETTA: Well, we . . . we hit the river. And it was quite an impact. The plane stayed together. Probably a lot of folks were worried it might split up, but it didn't. And it was sort of floating with the nose kind of sticking out. And people were very orderly. There wasn't really a lot of panic. And we made it out the exit doors on to the wing. And then people were trying to make their way to the rafts that were extending from the plane's fuselage. A few people went in the water, but I think they all got out. And we just were really looking for the boats at that point and helicopters. You know, obviously, if you're going to crash a plane, the Hudson River's a good place to do it.

BLITZER: Yes, a lot of ferries, a lot of boats in the area. What was it like when he said, "Prepare for impact"? Did everyone brace? What did you do to prepare for impact?

BERRETTA: Well, I think a lot of people started praying and really just . . . just collecting themselves. It was quite stunning. We knew there wasn't a lot of time, because we were quite close to the ground at that point, and we could . . . we could tell that the descent was somewhat rapid. So, I think people were very quiet. And, really, we weren't sure if they were trying to make it for the runway [or] river. But right after he said, "Prepare for impact," it was pretty evident that we were not going to make a runway. I think that's when folks were . . . obviously, the intensity heated up quite a bit at that moment.

BLITZER: Well, when you hit the water of the Hudson River, was it a relatively smooth hit, or was it a . . . was it a pounding? What was that like?

BERRETTA: It was . . . well, it's hard to describe and compare it, because it's the first time I have been through it. But it was, I think, pretty intense. It didn't last long. But the river is very, very smooth. The pilot extended the flaps. I don't know if he put the gear down or not, but I will tell you, it was just a great landing. I was really expecting the plane would careen or flip over or break apart. And that obviously didn't happen. And it did just kind of jockey back and forth. And at that . . . you know, we weren't really sure how long that was going to last. It seemed like it lasted for an eternity. But then we were all making our way off the plane. And that was a relieving moment.

BLITZER: Did it feel like birds or a bird was sucked into that . . . one of the engines that caused this? Because that's the preliminary guess we're getting from the FAA.

BERRETTA: I didn't see that or witness that. And I was probably in a position to, as I was literally right behind the left wing and very close to the . . . obviously, it's a window seat. I didn't see or hear anything. I did hear the engine sort of flame out. It looked like it was either on fire or smoke was coming from it. You could smell the smoke. It wasn't clear if the right engine was functioning or not.

BLITZER: You were on the left side – you were on the left of the plane. And you could see that engine, where there was smoke and some fire. But could you see the other engine as well?

BERRETTA: No. I think, as far as I know, just the left engine was . . . was having trouble. So, I don't know what really is the story with the right engine.

BLITZER: And when you were taking off from LaGuardia, I don't know if you know if you were taking off to the west, the east or which direction you were actually heading. Do you have any idea?

BERRETTA: No, I don't, Wolf, actually. I know . . . I know we were heading to Charlotte, which was home, but I don't know which direction that we were actually flying.

BLITZER: Yes. We're showing pictures – a picture right now, a still photo from the Associated Press, Fred, of folks standing on the wings, after they have escaped from this aircraft. And they're clearly waiting for a boat to come rescue them. I assume you you were one of those folks.

BERRETTA: Yes. I was – I was standing on the left wing for a little while. And then it was evident that the rafts on the left side of the plane were filling up. So, I actually went back in the plane with . . .

BLITZER: Yes, we have . . . we're also showing . . . Fred, hold on a second. I want to tell our viewers what they are seeing. They are seeing passengers getting on some of these boats after they have been rescued, after they got off the aircraft. And now they're being brought – this is videotape courtesy of our affiliate WABC. They get off the plane, and then they get on to these boats. But go ahead and walk us through that, those few moments. That must have been terrifying.

BERRETTA: It was. It was very intense and an experience I hope I never – or any of us have to – experience again. But I'm just grateful to God. I think . . . I don't know for sure, but I think that everyone got off the plane. There were a few injuries, but I think everyone survived. And I think that's miraculous.

* * *

Wolf asked me a few more questions, but it was getting hard to hear him in the crowded room. After finishing my call with CNN, I continued pacing around and drinking coffee. Passengers were talking to each other, asking where they had sat on the plane, and if they were okay. The room was filled with excitement and tension. Some people were hugging and crying, but others sat expressionless, seemingly stunned into submission at the reality of it all.

Adam Reiss had given me his card and asked if I would join him in the CNN studios for a live follow-up interview. I really felt like just keeping to myself, but the prospect of getting away from the scene was appealing, and after giving my name to the authorities once again and having a brief interview with police, I headed out.

I could not believe the number of people standing around, surrounded by dozens of police cars, ambulances, and fire trucks, with lights flashing all over. The air was biting, but I didn't care. I was alive, and I could barely believe it. We had all survived, and the feeling of gratitude to God, the flight crew, and those who rescued us was unlike anything I had ever felt in my life.

As we made our way in a van to the CNN studios, once again I checked my BlackBerry, which had been receiving calls and emails nonstop. I answered one call, a reporter from National Public Radio, and I was immediately tapped into their live broadcast. I finished that call as I exited the van and entered the Time Warner building at Columbus Circle, and proceeded into the CNN studios.

When people working in the studio around the control rooms learned I was a passenger on Flight 1549, they greeted me with wide smiles, telling me how thankful they were we had all survived. These heartfelt handshakes and words of warmth made me all the more grateful. It felt odd, but pleasant, that people I didn't know were so happy to see me alive.

I made a quick call home and spoke again with Liz, telling her where I was and to turn on CNN. Then I found myself speaking again with Wolf Blitzer, this time in front of a camera on live television. I recounted the story again to the best of my ability, and was escorted back to the green room, where more coffee awaited me.

As the evening progressed, I was interviewed by Lou Dobbs on CNN and then Bill O'Reilly at Fox News. I recounted the story several times, answering the same questions, but all the while my mind was really somewhere else, a faraway place I had never been before – a distant place of calm and peace. It's hard to describe, but I think that if someone had come up to mug me on the streets of Manhattan, I would have just smiled and given him a hug. Having just stared down death and escaped, everyone and everything in the world seemed good to me.

* * *

CNN had arranged for me to stay at a hotel near their studios, as I had promised to do more interviews the next morning. It felt strange walking into my hotel room with nothing but a donated sweatshirt on my back, a wallet in my pocket, and my BlackBerry in my hand.

The emails kept pouring in from all over, with text messages from reporters around the world. I was wired from the caffeine and adrenaline, and as I entered my hotel room I just stood there in the quiet stillness, wondering if it had really happened.

I called Liz again and talked with her for a while, then began returning emails, feeling completely unworthy of the attention being paid to me, but incredibly thankful for each and every one. Friends from long ago had seen or heard me on television, and it almost felt as though I was attending my own wake. Each email, each gesture of thankfulness was a reminder of how good it was to be alive. Like a balm poured on an aching muscle, each digital smile helped soothe the shock that still lay hidden underneath. I kept typing over and over, "You have no idea how good it is to be reading this email!" And, "The statistics were not with us, but we had a great pilot in the left seat and God in air traffic control."

After my fingers could type no more, I turned on the news and tried to relax. The first image I saw was our plane, making a left turn, with the engine on fire, narrated by an amazed reporter who had just emerged from the Bronx Zoo. I could see the left side of the plane, the side I had been sitting on, and began living the flight all over again. The contrast between watching a video clip of the flight on television and having just endured it made it seem like a dream that lingered on after awaking.

I knew that, between the overdose of coffee and the intensity of emotion I felt there, there was no chance of falling asleep. It struck me then just to kneel down by the side of the bed and thank God repeatedly, like a child who did not possess the vocabulary for more sophisticated prayers. After lying on the bed for about three hours, in a state of half consciousness, I decided it was pointless to keep trying to sleep. I needed to be ready for another series of interviews beginning at six a.m., and then head to Teterboro Airport for the trip home at eleven. I showered, made my way downstairs, and hailed a cab.

While I was waiting to go on the air at CNN, a sharply dressed reporter, who looked vaguely familiar, stood nearby, smiling and chatting on his cell phone. It was the same reporter who had been at the Bronx Zoo, who had taken the only live shot of the plane right after the birds struck. I told him that I had seen him on the news the night before, and he walked me through his version of the drama. He asked me if I would conduct a live radio interview, right there as I was waiting, and I obliged.

After my last interview that morning, I walked out into the bright, cold winter day, stepped into a black car, and began the drive to Teterboro. A corporate plane awaited me and other company associates, who had also been on the flight, to take us home. As I entered the car, the driver asked if I wanted to read a newspaper and proceeded to hand me a copy of the *New York Post*. On the cover was a picture of our plane floating on the water. The "Miracle on the Hudson" had been officially etched into the headlines of papers all over the world.

The driver then started talking about the crash. "Can you believe it?" he said. And he kept going on about the event. I was too tired to interrupt him and wanted to be charitable, so I just sat there and listened.

Then he finally paused, and I said, "It is truly amazing we all survived."

"WE! You mean you were on that plane?" He nearly drove into the opposing lane as he glanced back at me in the rearview mirror.

"Yes, I was and just left Fox News and have been on the air all night practically."

We continued our conversation off and on all the way to Teterboro. I thanked him for the ride, then stepped out and made my way into the General Aviation terminal area.

Although I was not overly enthusiastic about stepping onto another plane quite yet, the desire to get home overcame my recoiling nerves. The pilots looked familiar to me, and I remembered flying with them on a business trip overseas a couple of years before. After they gave us a briefing of the flight ahead of us, and a description of the Gulf Stream V aircraft that would fly us to Charlotte, they asked if we had any questions.

"Please tell us," I replied wearily, "that there are no geese in the traffic pattern."

* * *

As the wheels touched down at Charlotte Douglas International Airport, I felt my mind begin to unwind and relax for the first time. I just hoped I could hold it together when I saw my wife and children waiting for me in the terminal. When I did see their smiling faces, I knew every moment thereafter could never be the same. After a six-person hug and multiple kisses, we headed home.

The answering service indicated that our voicemail could hold no more messages, and the backup machine, which kicks in automatically, was also full. Reporters from around the country had called in the dozens, as had many from distant parts of the world, such as Spain, Colombia, and Australia. The phone kept ringing, and I was amazed at the continuing interest.

There was something about this event, something that reached out and helped a somber world feel hope, even if it was for just a moment in time. It suddenly hit me, too, beyond the gratitude I felt for all of us surviving. As I stood on my front porch, watching the sunset, I could view it from a distance, as if I were outside of myself, and I could see the joy of it. It had been flowing through my blood in the immediate aftermath, in concentrated doses, and I could now finally perceive it, and my eyes began to water.

The minute-by-minute issues and problems of daily life seemed trivial on the other side of having faced death. I had been pushed through a door with 154 people I did not know, but who were now like soul mates, locked into my heart and bound together. Now my entire being, permeated with this feeling of sublime euphoria, had to slowly adjust back to the ordinary world. Over the days ahead, I suppose I could have related to one of the Apollo 13 astronauts, facing the reality that I could not maintain the elation of a miraculous, lifesaving event forever, and needing to come down to earth again.

CHAPTER 9

MIRACLE

*God is always almighty; He can at all times work miracles,
and He would work them now as in the days of old were
it not that faith is lacking.*

St. John Vianney (nineteenth-century French priest)

So was the outcome of Flight 1549 a miracle? Virtually
every media story said it was. Like many others, I found
myself ruminating over the various circumstances of the event
with that question in mind.

Those circumstances were certainly extraordinary enough to
set the stage for a miracle. Although bird strikes are somewhat
common, a double bird strike resulting in loss of thrust in two
powerful turbine jet engines is extremely rare. Statistical data
from a report written by the U.S. Department of Agriculture
in conjunction with data provided by the Federal Aviation Ad-
ministration regarding wildlife aviation strikes from 1990 to
2007 indicates less than two percent of strikes resulted in two
engines being hit. There were millions of flights in the same

time period, carrying billions of passengers. The odds of an oc-
currence of the events of Flight 1549 were almost nil.

When nature ends up being the culprit of any disaster, we
quickly label it an act of God, as if there were no other causal
agent to blame.

We each must answer this question for ourselves at some
point in our lives: do we choose to believe in a higher power and authority that governs the universe, or do we believe
that man alone is the supreme power in an otherwise random
world? There is of course no way to prove whether a miracle –
the extraordinary intervention of divine power – occurred with
Flight 1549. In fact, science might very well tell us that though
the flight was exceptional, there is nothing that cannot be explained by or attributed to man exclusively. If such an assertion
were made I would not spend much time debating it. I do
not believe there's any way to prove that something happened
aboard Flight 1549 that was outside the normal laws of physics
or nature. However, the event does pose the possibility of divine intervention, because of the way in which the specific and
unique events came together perfectly for it to happen at all. I
believe that most of us on the flight, and many who watched
the story unfold, considered the question in this way.

In my first interview on CNN, I said that I thought it was
miraculous that everyone had survived. In the weeks following
the crash, as I reflected on the events leading up to the flight,
and the amazing outcome, I was all the more convinced of divine intervention. So many things could have worked against
us: if Captain Sullenberger had turned to the right instead of
the left, if he had continued flying north for a few more seconds, if there had been watercraft crossing the river where we
needed to land. The list of what-ifs seems endless.

And what of the geese? If I am to hold myself accountable
to faith in an all-powerful Creator, who governs all things in
a mysterious way, I must believe they were allowed to hit the

plane and disable the engines. But why would God allow that to happen? Only God knows, but there are some conclusions that seem logical to me.

Although humanity has a certain dominion over the earth, and clearly can influence events in either a positive or a negative manner, we do not act in a vacuum. We share the seas with mammals and fish; we share the earth with wildlife of various kinds; and we share the skies with birds. When we choose to fly, we know there is always the possibility that nature may interfere with our plans, but we accept that risk and take our chances. It seems that the good produced by our exercising our intellect and skill in creating and piloting flying machines outweighs the fractional risk of harm. Planes frequently fly in bad weather and usually make it through, even in circumstances that are far more precarious than we would like to admit. Bird strikes are not uncommon, and mostly go unnoticed by the public at large. Nonetheless, as soon as we leave the ground bound for the air, we move into a domain that birds share with us. Statistically speaking, a double bird strike that completely disables an aircraft's engines will occur again, though it may be decades and millions of flights from now.

Still, we probably had a better chance of being killed by a rogue meteorite than of being in a fatal plane crash caused by a double bird strike. According to National Transportation Safety Board (NTSB) data records, the odds of being in an airline accident on one of the top twenty-five airlines are approximately one chance in 8.5 million. Moreover, of accidents that do occur the number caused by factors other than pilot error, mechanical failure, or weather is only one percent. Bird strikes would be included in this "other" category.

* * *

In my research after the flight, I also learned that my assumptions about the most dangerous segments of flight had been wrong. I had always believed the takeoff and climb phase was the one most prone to accidents. In actuality, it is the final approach and landing phase that historically have been more precarious.

One set of statistics I had contemplated briefly during the flight, and also later in an interview, related to aircraft water ditchings. I had guesstimated the chances of surviving a water crash landing at approximately fifty percent. As it happens, I wasn't far off: prior to Flight 1549, the actual historical survival rate of commercial airliners in a controlled water ditching was fifty-three percent. In the history of commercial aviation there are only a few cases of intentional water ditchings, and there is only one other instance in which everyone survived: a Russian Aeroflot jet that ran out of fuel and ditched in the Neva River near Leningrad in 1963.

Other aspects of Flight 1549 reveal what I could call "little miracles." Although it had been overcast all day over Manhattan, with a light snow falling – in fact, I had thought there was a good chance the flight would be delayed or canceled – just before the flight, the weather had cleared. If it had remained cloudy, or if takeoff had been delayed even an hour closer to dusk, visibility would have been significantly reduced, making the landing and rescue operation that much more difficult and increasing the chance of fatalities.

A further important consideration was altitude. The glide ratio – the measure of how far a plane can fly at a given altitude without thrust – was *just* good enough to allow Captain Sullenberger to clear the George Washington Bridge and make a controlled approach into the Hudson River. It was estimated that the double bird strike occurred between 2,700 and 3,000 feet. Given the rate of climb after takeoff, if the strike had happened just a few seconds earlier, the Airbus might not have been able to clear the bridge. Captain Sullenberger would have been forced to approach the Hudson from a far less desirable angle, or perhaps not at all, resulting in a catastrophic crash into the city.

Then there is the case of the river itself, and the regular water traffic crossing it throughout the course of the day. There happened to be no boats in the strip of water where we crash-landed. But, there easily could have been, forcing last-minute course corrections that would have led to a far less controlled water entry.

Along with good visibility and lack of water traffic, the winds were calm that afternoon, and the river was relatively smooth, with little or no chop. This contributed significantly to the airframe's ability to enter the water level and stay together upon impact. Clearly, the deftness with which Captain Sullenberger was able to enter the water was impeccable, given all he had to contend with, but likewise the conditions over which he had no control could not have been more favorable for him.

Then there is perhaps the most remarkable aspect of the crash-landing. Analysis from the NTSB investigation revealed that the plane hit the water at *three times* the force that it was designed to withstand in a water ditching, and that it had stayed intact even though the fuselage had been cracked, the left engine broke off the wing on impact, and the right engine was almost in shreds. The airframe must have been within milliseconds of breaking apart, but somehow managed to stay together.

While avoiding collision with other aircraft and watercraft, Sullenberger also glided the plane into the river in the general proximity of ferryboats. These responded in minutes, and demonstrated exceptional skill at maneuvering around the plane despite the river's strong currents. At one point there were at least six watercraft, of varying sizes, making their way within a few feet of the plane. The operations of the ferryboat pilots, the Coast Guard, and the New York City Police Department were directed in a coordinated way that could have made Steven Spielberg proud. The boats could have easily collided with each other, or struck the plane's wings, causing fuel to leak into the water. Yet it could not have worked better if it had been rehearsed a hundred times.

And what about the passengers and their behavior? Did they contribute in any way to the overall success of the rescue, or did they inhibit it? As a passenger myself and a firsthand eyewitness, I have to say emphatically that not only did we contribute positively, we were a key ingredient. Amazingly, even though the majority of the passengers knew we were crash-landing in the river, there was not widespread panic. For the most part, we all waited our turn to leave our seats, and most avoided wasting precious time to grab luggage or handbags. I observed passengers taking leadership roles, trying to calm others down, helping others get out of their seats, helping people who had gone into the water get back on the wings or in a raft. Don Norton and the other passengers who opened the exit doors over the wings did so with precision and dexterity.

The three flight attendants on board the plane performed their roles exceptionally well. Donna Dent, Sheila Dail, and Doreen Welsh kept cool heads and did what they could to facilitate an orderly evacuation. The courage and performance of Doreen Welsh, who was stationed in the back of the plane, was particularly noteworthy. She had to deal with a partially open rear door, which was allowing water to enter the cabin, even though she had a deep gash on her leg. Understandably, the section of the plane where the most organized chaos occurred was in the very back. These passengers were some of the last to exit and certainly experienced the most terror both during impact and immediately following. Most of the force of impact on the fuselage was on the back half of the plane, as that was where the plane initially hit the water.

First Officer Jeff Skiles found himself in a scenario no flight simulator could have prepared him to handle. He was forced to run through a checklist for a water-ditching procedure that normally started at 30,000 feet – not 2,000. He had seconds to work through the list, which was several pages in length and had to be taken in precise order. It included shutting down various electrical systems to prevent fire and other hazards, as well as setting the altimeter elevation to zero to create the correct pressurization in the cabin so the doors could be opened after impact.

Finally, of course, there was the performance of Captain Chesley Sullenberger. A man with forty-one years of flying experience, a glider certificate, fighter-pilot training, and a mind for risk management and safety – no better pilot could have been sitting in the left seat that day. Perhaps the most important reason for the successful outcome was the decision process that Captain Sullenberger went through. From my own pilot training, which can hardly compare to Sullenberger's, I know that pilot error is usually caused by poor decisions or neglect, not mediocre execution. Many of the most horrendous air disasters in history resulted from bad decisions on the part of a single pilot, confounded by desperate circumstances or other contributing factors. Following the exceedingly rare event of a double bird strike in both engines, Flight 1549 was set up to produce all sorts of bad pilot decisions resulting in a range of potential catastrophic outcomes. But Captain Sullenberger coolly made only the right choices.

Air traffic control, doing their job well in immediately giving Captain Sullenberger clearance for LaGuardia and then Teterboro, did all it could to help. New York TRACON, LaGuardia Tower, and Teterboro Tower rose to the occasion and coordinated marvelously to give Captain Sullenberger several possible runway options. They of course knew that, as pilot in command, only Captain Sullenberger could make the final decision. The final and accountable authority for the successful operation and flight control of any airplane is always the pilot.

He has the right to override or ignore any instruction from air traffic control if warranted under the circumstances, as only he can determine the most optimal course of action for any specific scenario.

Flight 1549 was no different. Captain Sullenberger executed flawlessly at each stage of the flight. Immediately after the double bird strike, he assumed control of the aircraft, and First Officer Jeff Skiles instantly yielded his command and proceeded to attempt to restart the engines. These men must have been badly shaken after just witnessing the windscreen fill up with dark brown flocks of geese, and the resulting loss of power coupled with various warning sounds and lights had to be incredibly alarming to them. Yet they did exactly what they should have done with no wasted time, and worked together as one team in the midst of chaos.

The mental process that Captain Sullenberger then followed was the single most relevant factor in the flight outcome. Once he had assumed control of the aircraft, he leveled the nose immediately to regain lost airspeed, and began to evaluate options by communicating precisely and only as needed with air traffic control. His attention would have been focused on altitude, airspeed, and distance to various runway options. The all-important glide ratio weighed on his mind, as he knew that in that single metric of aircraft performance lay their destination. He systematically ruled out LaGuardia, as he was moving away from it and descending all the while, and then considered Teterboro. He then deduced that his glide ratio and descent rate were not optimal for any airport, considering the high risk of undershooting and losing all lives on board (and, potentially, many on the ground). Captain Sullenberger had to make his final decision in less than two minutes, and he knew that once it was made there was no turning back. He would seal the fate of all on board with that decision – a decision only he could make and one he would have to deal with for the rest of his life, if in fact he survived.

It is this all-important moment that every well-trained pilot knows is the ultimate test of skill and performance. From my meager experience as a private pilot, I can relate well to what the captain must have been feeling. There is a deep rift that runs through your body, an all-encompassing feeling of sickness and weakness that passes through your nerves. It intensifies as the situation continues and escalates in seriousness, and you have to fight it back with every bit of will you can muster. The temptation to go numb is always there, lurking in your mind, which is fighting to escape from the reality of unfolding events. You don't have time to think about a lot of things, and if your mind wanders for an instant, it can set up a chain reaction that may very well lead to disaster.

Captain Sullenberger must have experienced all these feelings at once, perhaps some subtle and others strong, but he probably knew they were there, waiting for him to give in. But he fought off all the demons of fear and shock and gut-wrenching uneasiness that only a pilot who has faced an emergency can understand, and he conquered them all masterfully. He ruled out LaGuardia and Teterboro, and he settled on the only option that seemed plausible – the Hudson. He maneuvered the plane over the river, picking a spot that was free of crossing watercraft but near passenger boats, and his entire mind and will must have been concentrated on making the most controlled approach possible. He knew it had to be the best landing of his life, keeping airspeed in a certain range, avoiding a stall, and ensuring that the wings were perfectly level as he let the plane enter the water. He had to do all this knowing that he could only control the first half of the operation, and that control of the rescue would be up to others.

In an interview that aired on *60 Minutes* with Katie Couric, when he was asked how he felt after realizing the plane had been damaged by a massive bird strike, Captain Sullenberger said, "It was the worst sickening pit-of-your-stomach, falling-through-the-floor feeling I've ever felt in my life. I knew immediately it was very bad."

Notwithstanding that overwhelming feeling, Sullenberger overcame and performed as near perfectly as possible. His actions and the water landing will be studied by all serious pilots and aviators for decades to come. He lived by the adage, "There are no old, bold pilots," and he brought all of his experience to bear on a singular, finite set of moments in which the balance of 155 lives hung in the air, quite literally. All pilots can learn something from him, and I hope they will.

In my own history of flying on commercial airlines, I recall only one occasion when I experienced first-hand the egotistical tendencies that can overcome a pilot. We were waiting on the tarmac for a long time in the heat of a summer day; a storm system had delayed all departing traffic for over an hour. It was pre-September 11, when the cockpit doors were left open prior to takeoff. The plane was an aged DC-9 that had seen too many years of flying, and it was full of unhappy passengers. I sat in coach in an aisle seat, and a rather robust man was sitting next to me in the middle seat. I could tell it was very uncomfortable for him, so I got up to see if there were any open seats in first class. There was one left, and I asked the flight attendant if it would be okay for the man in my row to move to that seat, given the long wait and uncomfortable temperature in the cabin. She did not receive my request well, indicating that it would *not* be okay.

Just before I turned around to go back to my seat, I noticed the captain standing in the galley on his way to the cockpit. I was tired of sitting, and since I was an avid aviation buff, I asked him a few questions about the delay. He told me that the storms were very bad over our route, and he did not like the initial vectors air traffic control had given him, so he had decided to wait to get ones that were more direct. I could tell by his manner and somewhat irreverent tone that he clearly was upset with air traffic control.

Sometime later, the pilot came over the intercom to say we had finally received clearance, and we took off. He told us the ride was going to be a "little bumpy." Indeed, that was the understatement of the decade: all the way to our destination, we flew just over the storm system. I could barely see the wing-tip lights flashing, and the plane kept rolling, sliding, and falling as though we were a toy in the hands of a toddler. Most passengers were very tense and scared, and I must admit myself that it was a strain on the nerves. I pondered our predicament and thought how unfortunate it would be if the plane broke apart in that storm and we all died because of a risky decision on the part of a frustrated pilot with an ego.

Captain Sullenberger, on the other hand, demonstrated the world-class demeanor and professionalism we hope for every time we step onto an airliner. He was the right man for the job, and while there may be other pilots who could have performed similarly, history must record with precision the overarching excellence Sullenberger demonstrated. His actions can serve as an example to us all, no matter what our individual vocations may be. When I told him right after the crash that he was a hero, and thanked him for saving us all, I knew then that he was not only an exemplary professional, but also a man of humility and grace.

* * *

About a week after the crash, *60 Minutes* hosted a reunion for the Flight 1549 passengers in Charlotte with the flight crew. I received an email from a work colleague asking if I wanted to contribute something to commemorate the event, something that would include pictures or sentiments, and would be given

to Captain Sullenberger. So I decided to write a poem for the
occasion:

> Azure blue skies and a quiet wind,
> One hundred fifty-five souls strapped in,
> The last leg for many, a new journey for all.
> Pushback, taxi, a wait, then the roll,
> A picture-perfect takeoff into the cold pure air,
> Five hundred, one thousand, two thousand – Then!
> A majestic formation where it should not have been,
> From any other vista, a beautiful sight,
> Yet one that would cripple the newborn flight,
> The sound and jolt of explosion and fire,
> Rocking, jockeying, confounding the peace,
> A decision and a call, a decision to make
> On the part of one, on the part of one, but for all.
> A decision to make quickly,
> Where, oh where could we glide our fall?
> A runway ahead, too far, too far,
> A runway behind, but too low, just too low.
> A river lay there, a blue strip of life
> Or maybe death, but no other option,
> Too little time to run the checklist, just too little.
> Fifteen hundred, extend the wings,
> One thousand, no time for past dreams,
> Five hundred: "Brace for impact,"
> Then the eternity of moments began for those in back,
> Fear, regret, sorrow, but still hope and prayer,
> Forty years of flight for him for this to prepare,
> Such a serene view of the great city,
> Thirty seconds to impact …
> A veteran co-pilot, obedient, steady and true,
> Three brave attendants, hoping for work yet to do,
> Twenty seconds to impact …

Messages to loved ones and calls to Heaven above,
Pleas for mercy for the white-blue dove,
Ten seconds ...
And two unseen angels sent to each wing,
To aid the Captain's seasoned hands,
"Be gentle to us, Hudson, be gentle and kind,"
The silent cry of those on board,
One second ... IMPACT!
The jolt of the river, like a roar of force,
Midst the rushing sound of an unlikely waterfall,
Then ... just silence ...
Intact! Alive! floating adrift,
One more command: "Evacuate!"
And the boats of life came, steered by pilots of skill,
Once all were safely off, a last task to perform,
Two walks down the battered plane now worn,
A sigh of relief, but to the world just calm,
A doff of his cap as the boat headed on,
One last glance at the slowly keeling ship,
One wing just in the air, as if to say farewell,
And as the sun bequeathed its fading glory to night,
The Lady of Liberty looked on, casting her shadow
Of light over the gray hues of rolling waters,
And the elation of life spread around the world.

The reunion was incredibly uplifting, filled with tears on the part of many, hugs, and repeated retellings of the tale. Many of the passengers and even the camera crew commented on how miraculous the whole thing really was. I had always believed in miracles, but somehow I never thought they could happen to me.

* * *

In the aftermath of Flight 1549, as with all plane crashes, controlled or uncontrolled, there were many important questions to investigate. The NTSB investigation confirmed that Captain Sullenberger and First Officer Skiles acted with precision, skill, and good judgment. For those of us on the flight, no report is needed to confirm this. The passengers and first responders likewise deserve credit. But what about the hand of God?

On occasion I have been asked that question. It, of course, is almost impossible to prove the action of God, even when it seems obvious. Science, when faced with miraculous cures, incorrupt bodies of saints that are decades or centuries old, or radical, positive changes of the heart of man when he decides to embrace faith or change his life for the better, ultimately can offer no explanation – precisely because these things are outside the dominion of science.

As a man trying to do what he can to live his faith, and realizing how far I must travel to become who I am meant to be, I must embrace the difficult questions. Why did God allow this to happen? He knew the birds would be in our flight path after takeoff. He could have "moved" them without a soul in the universe knowing. The flight could have taken off a few seconds earlier or later and missed the birds altogether. Yet we were allowed to hit them, and the close-to-catastrophic consequences were allowed to occur. Why?

Certainly God gives mankind great freedom and liberty to exercise decision, and sometimes this leads to potential disaster. But Flight 1549 was not a case of man allowing his ego to get the best of him and acting imprudently, as is the cause of many air disasters and other accidents. The captain did not choose to fly into dicey weather; the engines did not fail due to shoddy maintenance procedures to save costs; no, in this case, when man and nature collided – literally – it was not due to human sin, error, or any choice.

I believe that God took mercy on our flight, and I believe that all the prayers said in those surreal moments, by passengers, by onlookers, and by me, through the mysterious connection between human intercession and God's grace, saved us all. Any objective reasoning of the confluence of "luck" and series of circumstances that went in our favor, when the statistics clearly were not, would lead even the skeptical mind to conclude something unusual was at work: something profound, something extraordinary.

* * *

On the morning of February 13, 2009, during my first business trip after the crash, I had my first bad day. I was putting on my tie in a hotel room and I had turned on the television to catch the news just prior to heading out for a 7:30 a.m. meeting. The first image on the screen made me slowly reach out for the edge of the chair and sit down in a drained silence: dark smoke and a fireball filled the screen. I read the words in disbelief, "Continental Flight 3407 crashes in Buffalo," and those words crushed the euphoria I had been living in for nearly four weeks. "Survivor's guilt" spread over my whole being. The fire and smoke of the visual image penetrated me with a somber gloom and great sorrow. A small commuter plane, carrying fifty souls and manned by an inexperienced and fatigued flight crew, had crashed just prior to landing in heavy ice and bad weather conditions.

Within moments, my cell phone rang: it was a reporter in Charlotte who wanted to get my reaction to the air disaster. It was difficult to form words. Then I sat motionless for thirty minutes in disbelief, just staring at the screen, not wanting to move, and not understanding.

I was faced then with the most difficult question of all, the one that had been lurking in the background of my mind and which now suddenly sprang upon me like a lion in the night. It was the question I could have no certain answer to, but the one I had to face: why did God spare *us*? I did not want to consider this question. But if I wanted to believe God had a hand in the outcome of Flight 1549, then it would be hypocritical of me to reject it.

But how do I approach this question? How can anybody? For me, it's like the other difficult questions that mankind faces: why is there evil in the world, why must small children die, why must some endure tragic illness or misfortune, why are there those in the world who seek to kill others because they do not share the same mentality, why is there suffering in the world, why do bad things happen to those who try to do good – why was God Himself rejected, tortured, and crucified? Why is the simple message of Christ – to love, forgive, and sacrifice for others for the sake of God – hated by so much of the world? All these questions lead to the same answer, the only plausible one: God allows tragedy to occur (or miraculously intervenes to prevent it) *for the sake of a greater good.*

For me personally, the event imparted with precision and clarity the power of the promises of devotional prayer. God spared us because a greater good must come about, and He is counting on that. A confluence of efforts and circumstantial elements came together on Flight 1549 to create a very unlikely – a miraculous – outcome. It was the combined work of man and God in cooperation that allowed the flight to end as well as it did. There is simply no other explanation.

But a greater good from it must also come about. I cannot speak for others on the flight (though I believe God has a greater good for each of them), but as for myself: I feel I owe a debt that cannot be repaid. For all those who have not been as fortunate in plane crashes, I must remember them, I must pray for them and their families, and I must never take a moment for granted.

Flight 1549 was a life tutorial for me. Packed beneath the layers of dread, terror, hope, and euphoria, lay many lessons. The greatest was the renewed conviction of heart I experienced, as childish or simplistic as it may seem, in the trust of the great power of God to save and protect those who reach out to Him with a contrite heart and a knowing love.

I did not merit the gift of being spared in Flight 1549, but it was not my merit that mattered, it was only God's. This was the elixir that warmed and cleansed my soul in the frigid waters of the Hudson that day. For me there were two miracles on January 15, 2009: the first kept the skies clear, the waters calm, and a pilot's hand steady; the second was my interior resolution, moved by grace, to accept the outcome with *hope*.

CHAPTER 10

LESSONS

My longing for truth was a single prayer.

St. Edith Stein (Carmelite nun,
martyred at Auschwitz on August 9, 1942)

*T*he days rolled on, and the sequence of life inevitably had to adjust back to something like normal. Yet the question haunting me was: What would I make of my life now? Having been given a second chance, could I just revert back to who and what I had been before? Could it be possible to compartmentalize the whole event as just a rather dramatic and interesting chapter in my life? Could I go on with the same attitude and perspective?

No. That was the only plausible answer. To remain the same person would be a flagrant defiance of the reality of what had happened and of the great gift that had been given.

But although I could articulate that answer in my mind, and I could tell it to the world around me, I knew I had to begin to process what it meant, in my mind and in my soul. What did God want me to learn from His miracle? The lessons must be there, beyond the clear, deep thankfulness I could not express in words.

I know that the experience of Flight 1549 gave me the opportunity to contemplate my spiritual battles and my previous view of my life. I see clearly now the ways in which God was trying to get my attention, in both good times and bad – in my past successes and achievements, in my failures and family crises, in the deaths of my son and father. Even when I tried to make an authentic effort to respond to God's call, never was it wholehearted. I can see now that I kept something back from God – mainly, my total trust in His will and mercy. God understood me fully all the while: my struggles and my weaknesses, my intentions and my desires. But I was unwilling to let go, to make a complete commitment of my whole self, because I lacked the faith and trust to take that step. As when Peter faltered, watching Christ walking toward him on the water, I did not fully believe that God would supply me with the peace and rest I had sought all my life.

After making my New Year's resolution to improve my spiritual life, I had tried to strengthen my commitment. I can see that God was laying the groundwork in my heart for the events of January 15. Off and on for the previous fifteen years, since my reentry into the Catholic Church, I had struggled with praying the Rosary, for instance. It only takes about twenty minutes to pray through five decades. I seemed to face so many challenges when I tried to pray them. Inevitably, I fell away from it, and in retrospect, I realize now that I never approached it with the same effort that I put into so many worldly things.

As I began to recommit to the Rosary, I relearned the fifteen promises traditionally associated with it. I wondered if these could be true, and I said a prayer to God asking if indeed they were. The first promise was that one would receive "signal graces." And what on earth is a signal grace? I learned that a signal grace is a sign from God that confirms us or warns us of a path or action we have taken.

The only possessions I had with me after the crash landing were the clothes I was wearing, my BlackBerry, my wallet, a Rosary, and the old copy of the Pietà prayer booklet I had placed inside my shirt pocket, and of course my boarding pass. When I pulled the boarding pass out of my shirt pocket, I decided to keep it as a reminder of how fortunate I was to be alive. I placed it inside the prayer booklet and did not look at it again for several days.

After finishing the Rosary one afternoon a few days later, I thought I would look through the Pietà booklet and say a few prayers from it. When I opened it, I saw my boarding pass, and something struck me about it. The number fifteen was all over it: The flight number was 1549, boarding at Gate 15 at 2:15, departing on January 15. Then, I noticed other instances of this number. There were 155 passengers on board the plane. The traditional Rosary devotion comprises fifteen mysteries. The entire flight took place during the 3 o'clock hour, which is the fifteenth hour by military time. The plane hit the water at 15:31, and I stepped onto the ferryboat at 15:46 ET, when I received a call from my assistant. For me, the period from crash landing to rescue lasted fifteen minutes. I called my wife at 15:47. I must admit I was intrigued by this numerical coincidence, and I wondered if that was the signal grace confirming my question as to the validity of the fifteen promises for those who prayed the Rosary with sincere devotion.

According to the diary that Saint Faustina kept from her private revelations with Christ in the 1930s, she was told that the three o'clock or fifteenth hour is "the hour of great mercy." It was during this hour that the heart of Christ was pierced by a lance, and blood and water gushed forth as a fountain of mercy for the world. "In this hour," He told her, "I will refuse nothing to the soul that makes a request of Me in virtue of My Passion."

For me these coincidences were too overpowering to ignore, and I have found great consolation and peace from my devotion to the Rosary ever since the crash. The Miracle on the Hudson was for me a larger signal grace, confirming that I must commit to God fully, and live my faith wholeheartedly; doing the best I can in life in all I do and leaving the rest to God.

* * *

One evening a few days after the event, I decided I would try to look up the author of the book I had been reading on the plane just before the engines failed. I found Vinny Flynn's website and clicked on the email address to send him a note of thanks.

"I just want you to know that your book gave me comfort as we were going down," I wrote, "and for that I am grateful. I know a lot of people prayed on that plane, and I believe the Miracle on the Hudson was a testament to the mercy of God, and a sign of hope."

Vinny's response was kind, and we exchanged several emails in the following days that helped me deal with the aftermath. During the course of those days, and in part because of Vinny's insights and encouragement, I realized that something had changed dramatically for me in a spiritual sense. I felt that many of the personal demons that had plagued me before, that had been there to chide me and constantly tempt me from pursuing a more committed Christian life, were gone. It was very hard to describe, but in another email to Vinny I tried to explain how I felt:

    I will just go step by step and see where this
    takes me. I learned in the last minutes of that flight

that in an inexplicable way all my silly notions of being in control of my life are now like broken shells at the bottom of the sea. I was never at the helm, even though I really thought I was. But now, like the co-pilot who immediately gave the flight controls to the captain when the command was given, I must say to God: "not mine, but your life to lead." I must not forget these words.

He described His mercy as an ocean. I know that one can only be baptized once, but I have to tell you, in the currents of those cold waters, wet and frozen, kneeling on a jet wing, having faced death, I was baptized all over again.

And one of the messages of your book was just what you have said: Stay close to Him, stay close to Him in the days to come, there where the Heavens meet the earth in the greatest mystery of the ages. That will be the secret that I must live, but it can be no secret.

* * *

I look back on Flight 1549, and I think of the joy the families of the passengers felt when they learned their loved ones were safe. I think about the courage I witnessed on the part of many passengers, aiding and consoling those in need before and after the crash. I recall the skill and diligence of the ferryboat pilots as they rushed to our rescue, knowing we had such little time to be saved. I reflect on the decisiveness of the air traffic controllers, doing all they could to give Captain Sullenberger options, and how sick they must have felt inside when radar contact was lost. I think about the crew of Flight 1549, their professionalism and humility. I look back at all the people who came to our rescue – the medics, police officers, firemen, Coast Guard, and on and on. I think about the side of humanity

I saw that afternoon, and I know the greatness that man is capable of when put to the test and supported by the grace of God.

In the grand scheme of things, one might say that Flight 1549 was a relatively small event. In the end, it will be recorded as a rare bright moment in a list of tragic airline accidents. Its deeper personal significance must be left to each of us to contemplate and try to understand. Our own consciences must process the triumphs and travails of life and take from them what we may.

In the aftermath of the event, I often walked around my home, gazing at my children, dwelling in an almost ethereal contentment. I read long ago, in a book by a forgotten spiritual writer, about "living in the present moment with God." I was not really sure if I had ever experienced that feeling. One afternoon, after finishing a jog around our neighborhood, as I watched my children playing with our dogs, frolicking in the yard, on a cool, clear winter's day, I realized then just how important and irreplaceable each moment is. I knew I could never approach life from the same perspective again. The internal struggle I had so long felt, and which was almost a permanent part of me, was gone. In a few brief moments on Flight 1549 I made a decision that was irrevocable. It took all I had to say those words, and I know it was only grace, unmerited by me, that enabled me to say them.

* * *

There were other lessons for me in the aftermath of Flight 1549, and over the course of the weeks that followed I began to perceive them. I had been given so much in my life. The mercy of God had always been with me, and my meager faith had so many times been rewarded, yet I lacked the appropriate level of thankfulness and humility that God had desired of me. He of course did not need my gratitude to make His relevance or glory increase. He only wanted it for me so my faith could become more open to His workings; so that I might seek fulfillment in the only place it truly exists: in Him.

I began to see how the trials I had undergone in my life were made much harder by my lack of trust in the providence and generosity of God. Wherever I had made mistakes, it was because of my own pride – trusting too much in myself to get me through life's ordeals. I had always felt the loving invitation of God to abandon myself to Him, to yield to His will for me, and I knew that I'd held something back and was always afraid to admit it. On top of all that, I'd had the sacraments of the Church and their great rejuvenating power available to me, yet I had too often let their effects go wasted. The spiritual life, like all good things, requires commitment and discipline, and I had faltered on both fronts. Since perhaps what was the singular most humble act of my life, which was the contrite prayer I prayed on my knees as a young adult so long ago, God had been far more generous with me than I had been with Him.

Prior to my initial conversion, like the prodigal son I kept myself far from God my Father. After my conversion, God had given me glimpses of truth for which I did not show enough gratitude. He had nourished and uplifted me with the mystery of His word in Scripture. He had opened me up to the profound wisdom, logic, and necessity of the teachings and traditions of the Church. He had allowed me to participate in the power and serenity of the sacraments: the patience and mercy of God in Reconciliation; the intimacy of God in marriage; the unique and special presence of God in the Eucharist. All this sublime beauty of God's revelation through the Church I too often just squandered away due to the fatigue of the daily life battle, made so much harder by my own inner pride and lack of spiritual courage.

God went to great lengths to seek my attention, in my successes and my failures, in my joys and sorrows, and I was not brave enough to take that next step, to move forward in total faith, until he led me to the point of death, and asked me to walk out on a jet wing into frozen waters. He did not need to test me, but *I* needed it. Like Peter, who walked out on the water and looked down and lost trust, I realized in those moments how little faith I had really had in my life, but how much in return I had still been given. I understood more clearly the need for humility when approaching God: the simple requirements of sincerity, filial trust, and willingness to turn to the great reality of the depths of God's mercy with a contrite spirit.

* * *

I also had developed a profound appreciation for the virtue of prudence, for the importance of wise decision-making. We may think we all know how important making good decisions is in life, but too often we take this axiom for granted. Like Captain Sullenberger, who was tempted to make the more conventional choice between two airports that he could visually see, but ultimately chose the most unlikely third option of the river, I learned how critical is decision-making in life on all levels. There are always seemingly good options to choose, but there is always the best option – the one that will create the greatest good for those involved, and the one that will set up a chain reaction of positive momentum. Sometimes the best choice is not the one that feels good, or the one that the world around us would prefer us to choose.

Then there was the reality of mortality: death will come eventually, and it may be at any time. We see and hear of people who die suddenly, or from illness or accidents, and we often do not give much thought to when death will come for us. It is so easy to believe life will just go on, and death is far off in the distance. It is not easy to think about death, but I realized that it need not be something to fear, if we do our best to know, love, and serve God. I can tell you this from experience: when you are facing death, all you want is more time to prepare for it. To be ready is indeed a good thing.

Without question, one of the most personally uplifting and inspiring experiences in the whole event was my encounter with the dignity and contributing value of the human person. Flight 1549 was an ultimate success because of the combined efforts of so many different personalities and skills, from individuals of a vast array of diverse backgrounds and experiences. They all worked together on the afternoon of January 15, 2009, in an orchestration that for a few shining moments portrayed the nobility of humanity, guided and supported by the grace of God. I saw it in myself and in those around me. I know the bravest acts of my life were committed that day, and I was humbled and inspired by the actions and efforts of those around me. Chivalry is not dead, and it is just too bad that it too often takes a tragedy to bring this high form of virtue to the surface of man's being. I witnessed it that day in all of its forms, and am eternally grateful for that experience.

Finally, the most humbling and profound lesson for me was also the simplest, and the most difficult one to accept: God is in control. Without question, God is in control. It is such an easy mental path to believe that we have the greater dominion over our lives, and that God is somehow disinterested in our day-to-day activities. I realized with a rare clarity that God has, and uses, the ability to influence and work in us, through us and around us – but we often fail to see this divine action, or we actually inhibit it by our own actions and lack of obedience. We must do our part, put to use our talents and contribute what we can as responsible citizens for as long as we live, but in the end, we must let God do His part. We can't do it.

If we truly believe God created the universe out of nothing, we limit our life experience when we fail to also believe God cares about every detail and aspect of our lives. Scripture tells us the very hairs of our head are numbered and known to God.

Why then, do we worry so much? Why did I worry so much? It was my lack of faith. God led me through every trial and challenge of my life, and in a way this lesson culminated for me through His willingness and power to guide the myriad circumstances that allowed 155 souls to survive a sure catastrophe.

* * *

After several people encouraged me to write about my experience and how Flight 1549 had affected me and my life, I searched for a starting point that would take me back to the early days of my youth. Although the spirituality offered by *Jonathan Livingston Seagull* was not to be the ultimate destination for me, the book in a way served as a starting point for my spiritual journey (God through many means). If I were going to write, I felt a need to pay homage to it, because of the yearning for a higher purpose that it had imparted to me as a boy. I located the original paperback version on my bookshelf, waiting for me to open its pages once again.

As I reread the book in search of a few lines that would link it to my own story, there on page 86, I would of course find one more intriguing coincidence. I had forgotten that one of Jonathan Livingston's instructors was named Sullivan, whom he affectionately nicknamed Sully. I had never known or heard of another Sully in my life, until I sat in a television studio and was asked to verify a picture of Captain Chesley "Sully" Sullenberger prior to my interview. My immediate reaction when I saw this name in the book was of course to think of it as perhaps just an interesting coincidence. I smiled to myself and had to check my thoughts, because I knew that I no longer believed in coincidences.

EPILOGUE

My dream is of an island place,
Which distant seas keep lonely,
A little island on whose face,
The stars are watchers only.
And who would murmur and misdoubt,
When God's great sunrise finds him out?

From "An Island," by Elizabeth Barrett Browning

*A*s a boy, in my love affair with flight and dreaming of long-distance voyages on jumbo jets, I used to sit on the floor in my room and read through *National Geographic* magazines and marvel at the airline advertisements, usually found on the first few pages of each edition. The diagrams, featuring the air routes of various airlines to Europe, the Caribbean, and the South Pacific, were like dream-maps to freedom for me. I would study them and search for those faraway places on my globe. Somehow, in my mind the idea of flying to a distant tropical island became the ideal journey.

This dreamy notion was solidified for me when I read a poem in school by Robert Louis Stevenson called "Travel." As I read the first lines – "I should like to rise and go, where the golden apples grow, and where below another sky, parrot islands anchored lie" – I was hooked on the romantic notion of traveling to a distant isle. A few years later, I read *Robinson Crusoe,* and that helped transform my fantasy into something deeper, something more mysterious and alluring. The tropical island then became my mental escape, perhaps a defense mechanism that held the answers to my seeking soul and would lead me far away from life's issues.

On a business trip when I was in my mid-thirties, I was flying over the Pacific Ocean and had grown tired of dealing with a presentation I was working on. The in-flight movies did not seem all that appealing, so for the first time since I was a boy I picked up an issue of *National Geographic.* I found an article in it that described a South Pacific island called Palmyra. As the South Pacific had held a mystical appeal for me, I hoped to one day make a visit. For this trip, I would have to settle for the article.

I read that the lagoon-filled Palmyra Atoll, an incorporated territory of the United States, is less than five square miles in size and lies nearly a thousand miles south of Hawaii, part of the Northern Line Islands just above the equator. It is quite literally in the middle of nowhere. In World War II a passage was created in the atoll where ships could seek safe harbor. It remained uninhabited except for seabirds that migrate there for breeding, and occasional scientists conducting research. At the time, Palmyra was perhaps one of the last pristine islands in the world, unspoiled by mankind.

The beauty and serenity of this place struck me, and I decided to write about it as I sat there on my flight, wondering how far it might be out in the blue expanse I could see through my window. For some reason, I thought also about my spiri-

tual journey, my lifelong pursuit of truth, and there seemed
to be a connection I needed to make. Not having written a
poem in years, I felt strange sitting there at thirty thousand feet
and sketching one as the man next to me glanced through *GQ*
magazine, but I went ahead anyway.

"In Praise of Palmyra"

Deep, lush, peaceful, blue-green hues,
Little island in the Line,
Adorned in a silent swale
Of beauty almost out of time.
A pristine azure so alluring,
An ocean-aura like tanzanite,
Reflecting sun-swept tropic skies:
Diamond-white clouds, bright on bright.
Floating anchored, floating still,
Gems set in a sapphire sea,
A hidden treasure ever waiting
In the shade of crossed palm trees.
A channel carved, a hard-cut passage
Through the coral virgin garden,
So some may pass in sheltered-harbor
From battles yet fought, and those forgotten.
Of this isle's name, it is called Palmyra,
Far out in pacific distance,
Encircled by shoals of reef-rock
Guarding from storms of sudden instance.
What is to be of this isle-oasis?
Will its paradise on earth be known?
Will shipwrecked souls land here to find
Those leeward shores a replete home?
Of mine? Once lost in dark-deep waters,
Cold and tossed and drenched I cowered.

My strength emptied, my spirit gone,
In endless search of saving powers.
A shredded sail, a broken raft,
Existing on the swells of death,
Bailing, struggling, sinking often,
Nearly drowned with gasping breath.
My lifeboat drifted, listed, keeled,
A wayward soul in a great abyss,
But winds of truth steered my course,
And I found Palmyra, new life revealed.

When I wrote these lines, in a strange way they seemed to put closure on my initial search for resolution to the inner void I had felt in my youth and early adult life. At the time, I sensed I had matured inwardly, believing I had found the truth I had been seeking through my faith. But there was still a part of the mystery unresolved, like a tranquil waterway that suddenly comes to an end, without a clear passage in sight to finish the journey. There was something inside me yet unsettled, and I longed for it to be completed. In my own mind and heart and soul I had held something back, and I did not see it at the time.

As I reconsidered this metaphor in the aftermath of Flight 1549, I realized it was somewhat prophetic for me. For in the most unlikely of events, facing death but not giving up hope, with the simplest of decisions in the most challenging singular moment in my life, I decided to fully trust and let go, accepting God's will for me. I thought He was preparing me to die, but He was really preparing me to live. And that decision for me has indeed made all the difference.

Uniquely, we all search for our own Palmyra. The world tells us it might lie in countless places and things and pleasures and accomplishments. We each have our own ship to sail in this life, as we chart our course and make way in the open sea of our futures. We are urged on to do our best to make the most of what we have, using our talents and abilities to navigate the oceans and storms we inevitably encounter. As resilient and tough as we think we may be, even the very strongest need help from others and from God. The romantic notion of the self-made man really does not exist, for we know that every person who lives owes a debt to those who came before, a debt that is too large to repay. Besides our very lives, which we did not create and which are a gift, so much is provided for us along the way. When we discover something of great value, we should desire to share it; when we give in to the temptation to hoard it, it is lost. Even in the sharing of it, we do well if we do so with charity and humility, else the gift may go unreceived.

I have tried with sincerity to share something of value with you in this story, something that I cannot claim to own or even impart, but can only point to – and offer encouragement. Whatever your faith is, however small, large, or nonexistent, I invite you to assess your journey to your own Palmyra; to reflect where you are and where you are headed. And I would be remiss if I did not extend an invitation for you to visit mine.

Palmyra is easy to misjudge from a distance. It is not so small or isolated as one might think, or too idyllic to be real. There are people of every color, nation, and walk of life here, with room enough for a thousand more earths without ever becoming diminished. The journey is not so hard, and the caretakers of this island are ready to lead you through every obstacle you face, through that which would hinder you that lies in wait. Mary, the mother of Jesus and the Star of the Sea, will be a most expedient and trustworthy guide if you should choose her help, and you will find your way soon enough to the white shores, the gentle palms, and the aquamarine waters of life.

DEVOTIONAL PRAYERS

A General Prayer before Undertaking a Journey

O God, You called Abraham Your servant out of Ur and kept him safe and sound in all his wanderings. If it is Your will, protect Your servants. Be for us a support when setting out, friendship along the way, a little shade from the sun, a mantle against cold and rain, a crutch on slippery paths, and a haven in shipwreck. Bear us up in fatigue, and defend us under attack. Under Your protection, let us fulfill the purpose for our trip and return safe and sound to our home. Amen.

The Most Holy Rosary of the Blessed Virgin Mary

Begin with the *Sign of the Cross.*

> In the Name of the Father, and of the Son, and of the Holy Spirit. Amen.

Then say the *Apostles' Creed.*

> I believe in God, the Father Almighty, Creator of heaven and earth; and in Jesus Christ, His only Son, our Lord: Who was conceived by the Holy Spirit, born of the Virgin Mary, suffered under Pontius Pilate, was crucified, died,

and was buried. He descended into Hell; the third day He arose again from the dead; He ascended into heaven, and sitteth at the right hand of God the Father Almighty; from thence he shall come to judge the living and the dead. I believe in the Holy Spirit, the Holy Catholic Church; the Communion of Saints; the forgiveness of sins; the Resurrection of the Body; and life everlasting. Amen.

Say the *Our Father*:

Our Father, Who art in Heaven, hallowed be Thy Name. Thy kingdom come, Thy will be done on earth as it is in Heaven. Give us this day our daily bread, and forgive us our trespasses, as we forgive those who trespass against us. And lead us not into temptation, but deliver us from evil. Amen.

Say 3 *Hail Marys* for an increase in the virtues of Faith, Hope, and Charity.

Hail Mary, full of grace, the Lord is with thee; blessed art thou among women, and blessed is the fruit of thy womb, Jesus. Holy Mary, Mother of God, pray for us sinners, now and at the hour of our death. Amen.

Say the *Glory Be*.

Glory be to the Father, and to the Son, and to the Holy Spirit. As it was in the beginning, is now, and ever shall be, world without end. Amen.

Say the *O My Jesus*:

O My Jesus, forgive us our sins, and save us from the fires of Hell. Lead all souls to Heaven, especially those who are most in need of Thy Mercy.

Announce the First Mystery (see p. 116) then say the *Our Father*.

Say 10 *Hail Marys* while meditating on the first mystery.
Say the *Glory Be.*
Say the *O My Jesus.*

Announce the Second Mystery; then say the *Our Father,* 10 *Hail Marys, Glory Be,* and *O My Jesus.*

Announce the Third Mystery; then say the *Our Father,* 10 *Hail Marys, Glory Be,* and *O My Jesus.*

Announce the Fourth Mystery; then say the *Our Father,* 10 *Hail Marys, Glory Be,* and *O My Jesus.*

Announce the Fifth Mystery; then say the *Our Father,* 10 *Hail Marys, Glory Be,* and *O My Jesus.*

Conclude with the *Hail, Holy Queen:*
> Hail, Holy Queen, Mother of mercy, our life, our sweetness and our hope! To thee do we cry, poor banished children of Eve. To thee do we send up our sighs, mourning and weeping in this valley of tears. Turn then, Most Gracious Advocate, thine eyes of mercy toward us. And after this our exile, show unto us the blessed Fruit of thy womb, Jesus. O clement, O loving, O sweet Virgin Mary.
> V. Pray for us, O holy Mother of God.
> R. That we may be made worthy of the promises of Christ.

Follow with the *Prayer After the Rosary:*
> O God, Whose only-begotten Son, by His life, death and Resurrection, has purchased for us the rewards of eternal salvation, grant, we beseech Thee, that meditating upon these Mysteries of the Most Holy Rosary of

the Blessed Virgin Mary, we may both imitate what they contain and obtain what they promise. Through the same Christ Our Lord. Amen.

THE MYSTERIES OF THE ROSARY
The Joyful Mysteries:
To be meditated upon on Mondays and Saturdays.
1st Joyful Mystery: The Annunciation to Mary
2nd Joyful Mystery: The Visitation
3rd Joyful Mystery: The Nativity of Our Lord
4th Joyful Mystery: The Presentation of Our Lord in the Temple
5th Joyful Mystery: The Finding of Our Lord in the Temple

Not part of the traditional 15 mysteries. Added in 2002 by Pope John Paul II.
The Luminous Mysteries:
To be meditated upon on Thursdays.
1st Luminous Mystery: The Baptism in the Jordan
2nd Luminous Mystery: Our Lord's Self-manifestation at the Wedding of Cana
3rd Luminous Mystery: The proclamation of the Kingdom of God and the call to conversion
4th Luminous Mystery: The Transfiguration
5th Luminous Mystery: The Institution of the Eucharist as the sacramental expression of the Paschal Mystery

The Sorrowful Mysteries:
To be meditated upon on Tuesdays and Fridays.
1st Sorrowful Mystery: The Agony in the Garden
2nd Sorrowful Mystery: The Scourging at the Pillar
3rd Sorrowful Mystery: The Crowning with Thorns
4th Sorrowful Mystery: The Carrying of the Cross
5th Sorrowful Mystery: The Crucifixion and Death of Our Lord on the Cross

The Glorious Mysteries:

To be meditated upon on Wednesdays and Sundays.

1st Glorious Mystery: The Resurrection of Our Lord

2nd Glorious Mystery: The Ascension of Our Lord

3rd Glorious Mystery: The Descent of the Holy Spirit upon the Apostles

4th Glorious Mystery: The Assumption of the Blessed Virgin Mary into Heaven

5th Glorious Mystery: The Coronation of Our Lady as Queen of Heaven and Earth

The Chaplet of Divine Mercy

Our Lord appeared to a Polish nun, Saint Faustina Kowalska (1905-1938), and manifested Himself to her as infinite Mercy. He asked her to recite the following chaplet to invoke His mercy upon the world, saying:

"Whoever will recite [this chaplet] will receive great mercy at the hour of death . . . Priests will recommend it to sinners as a last hope of salvation. Even the most hardened sinner, if he recites this chaplet even once, will receive grace from My infinite mercy . . . Oh, what great graces I will grant to souls who will recite this chaplet."

To be prayed using normal Rosary beads

Recite one *Our Father*, one *Hail Mary*, and the *Apostles' Creed.*

On the Our Father Beads, say:

Eternal Father, I offer You the Body and Blood, Soul and Divinity of Your dearly beloved Son, Our Lord Jesus Christ, in atonement for our sins and those of the whole world.

On the Hail Mary beads, say:

For the sake of His sorrowful Passion, have mercy on us and on the whole world.

To conclude, say three times:

> Holy God! Holy Mighty One! Holy Immortal One! Have mercy on us and on the whole world.

Saint Christopher, Patron of Travelers

After being converted to the Catholic faith in the 200's, Reprobus, a stout man possessing immense bodily strength, built a hut beside a raging and dangerous river that had no bridge and decided to serve Christ by carrying wanderers across the river. He faithfully performed this task, night and day, whenever anyone had need of his service.

One night he heard a child calling to be carried across the river. Quickly he rose, placed the child on his shoulders, took his staff and walked into the mighty current. In the middle and the deepest part of the river, the child suddenly grew much heavier. "O child," Reprobus complained, "how heavy you are! It seems I bear the weight of the world on my shoulder." And the child replied, "You are correct! You bear not only the world, but the Creator of Heaven and earth. I am Jesus Christ, your King and Lord, and henceforth you shall be called Christophorus, that is Christ-bearer. When you reach the shore, plant your staff in the ground, and in token of my power and might tomorrow it shall bear leaves and blossoms." With these words, the child vanished.

Thereafter, Christopher became a zealous preacher and converted many to the Catholic Faith. He was eventually martyred by the Emporer Decius in 254.

> PRAYER IN HONOR OF ST. CHRISTOPHER
> Grant us, Almighty God, that while we celebrate the memory of Thy blessed martyr, Saint Christopher, through his intercession, the love of Thy name may be increased in us. Through Christ our Lord, Amen.

NOVENA TO ST. CHRISTOPHER
To be said daily for nine days

Almighty and eternal God! With lively faith and reverently worshipping Thy Divine Majesty, I prostrate myself before Thee and invoke with filial trust Thy supreme bounty and mercy. Illumine the darkness of my intellect with a ray of Thy heavenly love, that I may contemplate the great virtues and merits of the saint in whose honor I make this novena, and following his example imitate, like him, the life of Thy divine Son.

Moreover, I beseech Thee to grant graciously, through the merits and intercession of this powerful helper, the petition which through him I humbly place before Thee, devoutly saying, "Thy will be done on earth as it is in Heaven." Vouchsafe graciously to hear it, if it redounds to Thy greater glory and to the salvation of my soul. Amen.

O God, who didst make Saint Christopher a true Christ-bearer who converted multitudes to the Christian Faith, and who didst give him the grace to suffer for Thy sake the most cruel torments; through the intercession of this saint we implore Thee to protect us from sin, the only real evil. Preserve us, also against harmful elementary forces, such as earthquake, lightning, fire, and flood. Amen.

Great Saint Christopher, seeking the strongest and mightiest master, thou didst find him in Jesus Christ, the almighty God of Heaven and earth, and didst faithfully serve Him with all thy power to the end of thy life, gaining for Him countless souls and finally shedding thy blood for Him; obtain for me the grace to bear Christ always in my heart, as thou didst once bear Him on thy shoulder, so that I thereby may be strengthened to overcome victoriously all temptations and resist all enticements of the world, the flesh, and the devil, and that the powers of darkness may not prevail against me. Amen.

My Lord and my God! I offer up to Thee my petition in

union with the bitter passion and death of Jesus Christ, Thy Son, together with the merits of His immaculate and blessed Mother, Mary ever virgin, and of all the saints, particularly with those of the holy helper in whose honor I make this novena.

Look down upon me, merciful Lord! Grant me Thy grace and Thy love, and graciously hear my prayer. Amen.

Saint Joseph of Cupertino, Patron of Aviators

Saint Joseph (1603-1663) was a Franciscan friar who is most famous for his miraculous levitations which occurred during Mass, prayer, meditation, and even at the very mention of God or Mary. He was known to levitate for up to two hours at a time. Additionally, he spoke with animals, raised the dead, and cured the ill.

PRAYER TO ST. JOSEPH OF CUPERTINO

Dear ecstatic Conventual Saint who patiently bore calumnies, your secret was Christ the crucified Savior who said: "When I will be lifted up I will draw all peoples to myself." You were always spiritually lifted up. Give aviators courage and protection, and may they always keep in mind your greatly uplifting example. Amen.

Saint Michael the Archangel

PRAYER TO ST. MICHAEL

Saint Michael the Archangel, defend us in battle; be our defense against the wickedness and snares of the devil. May God rebuke him, we humbly pray; and do though, O Prince of the heavenly host, by the power of God, cast into Hell Satan and all the other evil spirits who prowl about the world seeking the ruin of souls. Amen.

THE CHAPLET OF ST. MICHAEL

A devout Servant of God, Antonia d'Astonac, had a vision of Saint Michael and was told to honor him by nine salutations to the nine Choirs of Angels. Saint Michael promised that whoever would practice this devotion in his honor would have, when approaching Holy Communion, an escort of nine angels chosen from each of the nine Choirs. In addition, for those who would recite the Chaplet daily, he promised his continual assistance and that of all the holy angels during life.

While making the *Sign of the Cross*, say:
> O God, come to my assistance. O Lord, make haste to help me. Then say one *Glory Be*.

By the intercession of Saint Michael and the celestial Choir of Seraphim may the Lord make us worthy to burn with the fire of perfect charity. Amen.
Say one *Our Father* and three *Hail Marys*.

By the intercession of Saint Michael and the celestial Choir of Cherubim may the Lord grant us the grace to leave the ways of sin and run in the paths of Christian perfection. Amen.
Say one *Our Father* and three *Hail Marys*.

By the intercession of Saint Michael and the celestial Choir of Thrones may the Lord infuse into our hearts a true and sincere spirit of humility. Amen.
Say one *Our Father* and three *Hail Marys*.

By the intercession of Saint Michael and the celestial Choir of Dominions may the Lord give us grace to govern our senses and overcome any unruly passions. Amen.
Say one *Our Father* and three *Hail Marys*.

By the intercession of Saint Michael and the celestial Choir of Powers may the Lord protect our souls against the snares and temptations of the devil. Amen.

Say one *Our Father* and three *Hail Marys*.

By the intercession of Saint Michael and the celestial Choir of Virtues may the Lord preserve us from evil and falling into temptation. Amen.

Say one *Our Father* and three *Hail Marys*.

By the intercession of Saint Michael and the celestial Choir of Principalities may God fill our souls with a true spirit of obedience. Amen.

Say one *Our Father* and three *Hail Marys*.

By the intercession of Saint Michael and the celestial Choir of Archangels may the Lord give us perseverance in faith and in all good works in order that we may attain the glory of Heaven. Amen.

Say one *Our Father* and three *Hail Marys*.

By the intercession of Saint Michael and the celestial Choir of Angels may the Lord grant us to be protected by them in this mortal life and conducted in the life to come to Heaven. Amen.

Say one *Our Father* and three *Hail Marys*.

Say one *Our Father* in honor of each of the following: Saint Michael, Saint Gabriel, Saint Raphael, and our Guardian Angel.

Conclude with:

> O glorious prince Saint Michael, chief and commander of the heavenly hosts, guardian of souls, vanquisher of rebel spirits, servant in the house of the Divine King and

our admirable conductor, you who shine with excellence and superhuman virtue deliver us from all evil, who turn to you with confidence and enable us by your gracious protection to serve God more and more faithfully every day.

Pray for us, O glorious Saint Michael, Prince of the Church of Jesus Christ, that we may be made worthy of His promises.

Almighty and Everlasting God, Who, by a prodigy of goodness and a merciful desire for the salvation of all men, has appointed the most glorious Archangel Saint Michael Prince of Your Church, make us worthy, we ask You, to be delivered from all our enemies, that none of them may harass us at the hour of death, but that we may be conducted by him into Your Presence. This we ask through the merits of Jesus Christ Our Lord. Amen.

The Guardian Angels

"For he hath given his angels charge over thee; to keep thee in all thy ways. In their hands they shall bear thee up: lest thou dash thy foot against a stone" -Psalm 9, 11-12.

"And there appeared to him an angel from heaven, strengthening him" - Saint Luke 22, 43.

TRADITIONAL PRAYER TO ONE'S GUARDIAN ANGEL

Angel of God, my guardian dear, to whom God's love commits me here, ever this day, be at my side to light and guard, to rule and guide. Amen.

PRAYER IN HONOR OF THE GUARDIAN ANGELS

O Almighty and merciful God, who hast commissioned Thy angels to guide and protect us, command them to be our assiduous companions from our setting out until our return; to clothe us with their invisible protection; to keep from us all danger of collision, of fire, of explosion, of fall and bruises, and finally, having preserved us from all evil, and especially from sin, to guide us to our heavenly home. Through Jesus Christ, our Lord. Amen.

May the almighty and merciful Lord lead us in the way of peace and prosperity. May the Angel Raphael be our companion on the journey and bring us back to our homes in peace, health, and happiness. Amen.